MW00647336

# The Race to the Dan

## *The Retreat That Rescued the American Revolution*

By

**Larry G. Aaron**

Halifax County Historical Society
Halifax County, Virginia

*The Race to the Dan*

ISBN: 978-0-9795258-0-3

*Cover*: A copy of an original watercolor by Don Troiani. Courtesy of
the Guilford Courthouse National Military Park.

Warwick House Publishers
720 Court Street
Lynchburg, Virginia 24504

# TABLE OF CONTENTS

The people of Halifax received us with the affection
of brethren, mingled with the admiration of the
brave devotion to country, just exhibited.

> —Light-Horse Harry Lee
> concerning the reception of
> Greene's army after crossing
> the Dan River, from 1812
> edition of his *Memoirs*

# Dedication

To the memory of
the late

Lt. Colonel Bill Lindley
U.S. Army Ret.

He served as President of the Dan River Chapter of the Virginia Society, Sons of the American Revolution. Through his well-known portrayal of a Revolutionary War Militiaman at Guilford Courthouse and other national military parks, Colonel Lindley's life greatly impacted the Patriotic, Educational, and Historical goals of the Society. His programs were popular in Alamance County, North Carolina, where his leadership assisted in establishing the monument to Pyle's Massacre. Colonel Lindley also participated in the first modern celebration of Greene's Crossing of the Dan in February 1999.

I have some expectation of collecting a
force sufficient in this country to enable me
to act offensively and in turn race Lord
Cornwallis as he has done me.

> —General Nathanael Greene
> to General John Butler,
> February 17, 1781, from
> Halifax Courthouse.

# Acknowledgments

Special thanks is due the Halifax County Historical Society for the publication of this book, and especially to Barbara Bass, its President and Vice-Regent of the Berryman Green Chapter DAR, for her work and guidance in preparing this manuscript for printing.

The cover picture is a reproduction of an early Don Troiani water-color, used with the kind permission of the Guilford Courthouse National Military Park.

Special thanks also to Kenneth Haynes of Reidsville, North Carolina, a local historian who has thoroughly studied Greene's campaign. He is responsible for the map used with the first article "The Race to the Dan" which appeared in the 1995 issue of the Sons of the American Revolution *SAR Magazine*. His expertise also aided in the accuracy of that narrative.

Some of the portraits of the principal combatants in the story are from the National Archives. The biographical section came primarily from *Appleton's Cyclopedia of American Biography*, six volumes, published in 1887-1889, and Benson Lossing's *Pictorial Field-Book of the Revolution*.

Win Williams, editor of the *SAR Magazine*, and Emyl Jenkins, editor of *Evince* magazine, both generously gave permission for the inclusion of articles from their publications. Dr. Dennis Conrad, editor of the *Nathanael Greene Papers*, also allowed the use of his remarks delivered in South Boston, Virginia, in 1999.

I wish to thank my compatriots in the Dan River Chapter of the Virginia Society SAR for their encouragement in this project. Each of our Revolutionary War ancestors served in some capacity in the various theaters of battle and we stand on their shoulders as we support the goals of the National Society of the Sons of the American Revolution.

I am grateful for the research assistance of Dan Shaw, Peggy Hammond, and Douglas Powell, and to Joe Hines, principal of Project Arts and Ideas, and designer of the Crossing of the Dan permanent exhibit at The Prizery in South Boston, Virginia. Joe's research of the Nathanael Greene Papers in the Clements Library at the University of Michigan uncovered the Cavalry Return images used in this volume with the kind permission of that library.

Additional appreciation is due award-winning Revolutionary War historian John Buchanan for previewing the manuscript and contributing the Introduction, and also to Virginia's Fifth District congressman Virgil Goode for graciously contributing the Foreword.

No words written in this publication can adequately convey or measure the contributions and sacrifices of the men in General Greene's army. The spirit of liberty that drove them to endure the most extreme hardships in their strategic retreat is the reason we celebrate the American Revolution. Theirs is a story that must be told and retold to future generations. We owe these men, and especially General Greene, our lives and our good fortunes.

Larry G. Aaron

# Foreword

The casual student of history knows that Lord Cornwallis surrendered to George Washington at Yorktown in 1781, thereby bringing a
successful ending for America in the Revolutionary War. Even some
noted scholars of United States history are not familiar with a key
event that took place in Halifax County, Virginia, on Valentine's Day,
February 14, 1781.

*The Race to the Dan*, which Larry Aaron has appropriately entitled
his book, paved the way for the colonial victory in Yorktown. Mr.
Aaron has researched and documented the events which included
Boyd's Ferry and Irwin's Ferry near what is now the town of South
Boston. At this juncture, the forces of General Nathanael Greene,
whom General Washington had placed in charge of American troops
in the southern colonies, were reenergized, refocused, re-enforced
and resupplied. South Boston and Halifax County today are known
for their gracious hospitality, and they rolled out the proverbial red
carpet for General Greene and his soldiers.

Lord Cornwallis had missed the opportunity to destroy the colonial
forces in the south by defeating them in battle before they reached
the Dan River. More battles followed, and General Greene with his
re-enforcements and new supplies, was able to prevail over the
British at Guilford Courthouse and several other places, forcing
Cornwallis to move toward Yorktown where the British forces
surrendered, as the band played "The World Turned Upside Down."

While the focus of so many of our history books is on Yorktown, we
should all be aware of what General Greene did in beating the British
in the race to the Dan River and securing safety on the north side of
the river. Cornwallis, because of General Greene, was unable to
claim that the southern colonies, including much of Virginia, were
firmly in British hands. One must wonder whether the French would
have helped from the sea at Yorktown if the British had been in
control of all of the South. Mr. Aaron had consulted many sources
and has drawn upon accounts and unpublished works to highlight the
importance of the Crossing of the Dan to our independence and

11

history. While colonial history can be a dry subject, Mr. Aaron has relied upon firsthand sources to draw his conclusions of the importance of this event in a readable style. His work should generate greater interest not only in Halifax County and Southside Virginia, but also around the country for the role that General Greene and his forces played in the winning of the Revolutionary War.

In addition to saluting Mr. Aaron for his work that is so appropriately subtitled, The Retreat that Rescued the American Revolution, the Halifax County Historical Society must be praised and thanked for its role in publishing *The Race to the Dan*, which should be read by the casual reader of history in addition to scholars of Revolutionary War and United States history.

Virgil H. Goode, Jr.
United States Congressman
Virginia Fifth District

# Introduction

Lieutenant General Charles, 2nd Earl Cornwallis, was livid. His light troops, the eyes and ears of his army, under his favorite officer, Lieutenant Colonel Banastre Tarleton, had been destroyed as a fighting force on 17 January 1781 at the Battle of Cowpens by American regulars and militia commanded by that master tactician, Brigadier General Daniel Morgan. His Lordship vowed to catch Morgan and free the prisoners. Thus began in that rain-soaked winter, over dirt roads that were quagmires by day and rock-hard moonscapes by night, a pursuit that Major General Nathanael Greene described as Cornwallis' "mad scheme."

Except for the final British defeat at Yorktown, the Southern Campaign is not as heralded as the campaigns in the North. But it was just as critical to the American victory and the establishment of an independent United States made up of the original Thirteen Colonies. Without victory in the South, the new nation might well have been comprised of the Northern States and the upper South, with Britain at least retaining South Carolina and Georgia.

The beginning of the end of the first phase of the Southern Campaign began at Cowpens. It had started with one British victory after another, but beginning in the early summer of 1780 a guerrilla campaign foiled the British attempt to establish control over the vast Carolina Back Country. That campaign bought the time necessary for a reinvigorated southern Continental Army under the brilliant strategist Nathanael Greene to once again place itself in harm's way. The first result was the British disaster at Cowpens. But the American numbers were too small to face Cornwallis' main army, and thus began the most famous retreat in American military history.

The final dash for the Dan River in Virginia was a tale of two armies within shouting distance of each other. But the Americans pulled off one of warfare's most difficult feats: retreat in the face of a rapidly pursuing enemy. It was described by Banastre Tarleton as "judiciously designed and vigorously executed." The army had been preserved, and one month later Nathanael Greene would lead his troops back across the river to engage Cornwallis in a bloody battle that would complete the ruin of His Lordship's army and lead to the American reconquest of South Carolina and Georgia.

The successful American crossing of the rain-swollen Dan River ahead of the British was one of the outstanding operations of the war and a key element in Greene's victorious Southern Campaign. It deserves wide recognition.

John Buchanan


John Buchanan is the author of *The Road to Guilford Courthouse: The American Revolution in the Carolinas*. He is currently writing a sequel to this book, *The Road to Charleston: Victory in the Carolinas*, which will cover the second half of the Carolina campaign.

Buchanan's other books include *Jackson's Way: Andrew Jackson and the People of the Western Waters*, published in 2001 and *The Road to Valley Forge: How Washington Built the Army That Won the Revolution*, published in 2004. *The Road to Valley Forge* was awarded the Thomas Fleming Award by the Philadelphia American Revolutionary War Round Table as the best book on the American Revolution published in 2004.

# Preface

This book has three basic goals. First, to familiarize the reader with the story of The Race to the Dan that concluded on February 13-14, 1781. Major General Nathanael Greene's American army crossed the river near South Boston, Virginia, thus ending one of the most dramatic events of the American Revolution.

Sadly, my studies of Virginia history and American history respectively in grade school and high school never mentioned it. I first learned about Greene's race with Cornwallis as I studied my family ancestry many years later. I discovered that my 8th great-grandfather, Abraham Aaron, shod horses, supplied beef and repaired guns for the continental troops, most likely after Greene's crossing of the Dan River. Also, his oldest son, Abraham Aaron, Jr., fought as a drafted militiaman at the Battle of Stono during the Siege of Charleston at the beginning of the Southern Campaign.

After this newly acquired information piqued my curiosity, I came across a small booklet by W. Carroll Headspeth and Spurgeon Compton of South Boston, Virginia titled *The Retreat to the Dan* published during the bicentennial anniversary of America's Revolution. I also became familiar with the story from the book *An Intimate History of the American Revolution in Pittsylvania County, Virginia* by Francis Hallam Hurt.

During my lifetime, I have read considerable amounts of war history, but I must confess that I find the Race to the Dan the most fascinating of all. I have given presentations about it to school groups, historical societies and museums, and a variety of other organizations. I can truly say that I never tire of talking about it.

Beyond the story itself is its significance. It is important to understand how the Race to the Dan factored into the overall conduct and consummation of the Revolution. Even though ten years after the event the story was fading from public memory, and histories of the war since then have frequently marginalized the event, General Greene's climatic crossing of the Dan River saved the Revolution just in the nick of time and set up a sequence of events that propelled Cornwallis toward Yorktown and surrender. In addition, it set the stage for Greene's army and partisan groups to reclaim the Southern Colonies, finally bottling up the British in Charleston, South Carolina. All this without winning a single battle. Of course, Greene's Crossing of the Dan was not the only great event in that war, but its importance is often overlooked in deference to lesser events that did not accomplish half as much.

Also, Greene's strategy was nothing short of magnificent, but has sometimes been ignored because his actions have always been tagged a retreat. Since retreating armies don't win victories, it has not been given the attention it deserves in histories of the war.

But what a retreat it was—Greene's strategy puts him in league with the great Roman generals of antiquity and quite honestly is the stuff of legend. How Greene's army brought a much more superior British army to its knees is a marvel. In fact, it is still studied by military strategists because America's recent wars including Vietnam have not only been conventional but insurgency-driven wars—just the kind Greene excelled at.

Besides the story itself, a second goal of this book is to promote the celebration of Greene's Crossing of the Dan River. To that end several articles have been included: namely, the address of Dr. Dennis Conrad, editor of the *Nathanael Greene Papers*, which was delivered February 13, 1999; an article on "The Prizery: Its Journey into the Past," which appeared in the Winter issue 2006 of the *SAR Magazine*; and the article "Crossing of the Dan 225th Anniversary Celebration" which appeared in the January 2006 issue of *Evince* magazine, a regional publication for which this author is Associate Editor.

The Prizery, an abandoned tobacco processing factory in South Boston, Virginia, turned community center, will host a permanent exhibit on Greene's Crossing of the Dan River. The Headspeth Window at the exhibit site provides an excellent view of Boyd's Ferry where part of Greene's Army crossed the Dan River. All funds from the sale of this book are designated for this exhibit.

A third goal of this book is to provide an extensive bibliography that will aid the reader in research on the American Revolution, especially the Southern Campaign. It includes both Ph.D. dissertation and Master's thesis listings, book sources for young people, plus sources for Revolutionary War era movies and music. Internet web sites listed, not only include great information, but offer links to other sites. Finally, a Revolutionary War timeline provides a ready reference to the chronology of events.

The year 2007 commemorated the 226th anniversary of Nathanael Greene's Crossing of the Dan, which helped bring the Declaration of Independence from idea to reality. Since then our country has become a military and economic superpower, a beacon for democracy around the world, and a giant in scientific and technological achievement. In 1969 our nation rallied its national spirit and put the first man on the moon.

But let us not forget, it was that same American spirit that rallied Greene's decimated army in the winter of 1781. The distance to the Dan River—230 miles away—may as well have been the distance to the moon. Yet, against all odds, Greene's army got there first. And that's a big part of the reason Old Glory flies proudly across the length and breadth of this land.

Larry G. Aaron

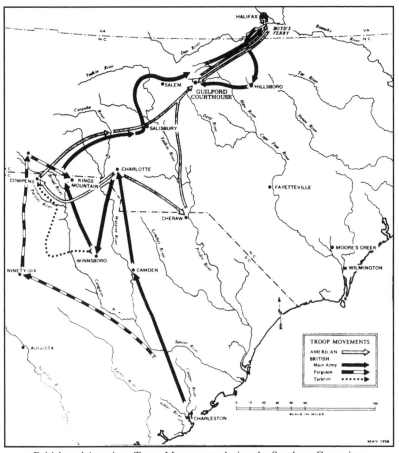

British and American Troop Movements during the Southern Campaign.

# Part I
## The Story

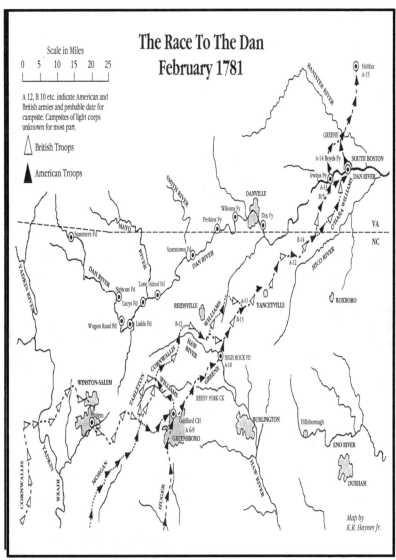

The Race To The Dan
February 1781

Scale in Miles
0   5   10   15   20   25

A 12, B 10 etc. indicate American and
British armies and probable date for
campsite. Campsites of light corps
unknown for most part.

△ British Troops

▲ American Troops

Courtesy of Kenneth Haynes.

# The Race to the Dan

February 14, 1781, dawned a cold and dreary day in the heart of a severe winter. Yet, that day marked a pivotal juncture in American history. By sundown the Race to the Dan was over, and the American Revolution had been rescued once again.

Crossing of the Dan
(Courtesy of the Guilford Courthouse National Military Park, National Park Service)

The next day—February 15—British General Cornwallis arrived at Boyd's Ferry on the Dan River in Virginia. Disbelief hung in the air like a dark cloud. Staring across the open water at Nathanael Greene's army, Cornwallis faced bitter disappointment. With a rain swollen river between them and all available boats on the other side, catching Greene's troops was now out of the question. The ragged and exhausted American army rested, safe and unreachable. So near, yet so far away.

Sitting atop his mount, Cornwallis surveyed his veteran British troops with some consolation. He hadn't lost a race; he had evicted the American army from North Carolina. Yet, he did understand that chasing Greene had been an exercise in futility, not to mention a logistical and tactical nightmare. Despite Cornwallis' best effort, the elusive, deceptive American general had managed to keep his force intact. Cornwallis well noted "Greene is more dangerous than Washington. I never feel secure when encamped in his neighborhood."

## *Cornwallis and Greene—A Study in Contrasts*

Lord Charles Cornwallis

Reflecting on the two antagonists reveals a striking mix of talent and personality. Educated at Eton and Cambridge, Charles, the Second Earl of Cornwallis, was high born, a powerful aristocrat seated in parliament. He opposed the harsh treatment of the Colonies, but once war broke out he sailed for America. Stocky in appearance and afflicted with a weak eye, the 42 year-old Cornwallis walked with a heavy plodding step, fought by the textbook, improvising but little.[1] Nevertheless he established a reputation for bravery and bulldog determination.

Nathanael Greene did not rise through the ranks as did Cornwallis. He was a Rhode Island Quaker, later expelled from their meeting for involving himself in the Revolutionary cause. His father, a leading minister in the sect, had little use for formal education, training Nathanael at the family iron foundry. But young Nathanael studied the military classics of Caesar, Turenne, and others. He quickly evolved into a military genius. Starting out as a private in the Kentish guards, less than two months later the Rhode Island legislature appointed Greene a Brigadier General in charge of three regiments. He became Washington's favorite general and designated successor. He served at Trenton, Brandywine, Valley Forge, and in other campaigns. At age 38—and just under six feet—Greene projected a buoyant disposition and a commanding appearance, even though he suffered with asthma, a continual eye infection, and struggled with a noticeable limp. He also had a reputation for losing battles. In his words, "We fight, get beat, rise and fight again." The enemy always paid more than it could afford for any "victory" against this master strategist.

## British Sweep Through The South

In 1778 a stalemate in the North forced the British to turn their attention to the southern colonies. Georgia was overrun. Cornwallis swept through South Carolina, assisting in the capture of Charleston, and devastating an American army at Camden. The British hoped this display of superiority would consolidate Loyalist support in the region. It didn't. After the Loyalists' defeat at King's Mountain in October 1780, Cornwallis canceled his first invasion of North Carolina.

What was left of the bedraggled American army that survived Camden received a respite from destruction as Cornwallis waited for reinforcements. On December 3, 1780, Major General Nathanael Greene took command of the Americans at their camp near Charlotte, North Carolina. He was taken aback when he saw the condition of his army. Miserable food and lack of clothing had caused an outbreak of dysentery, diarrhea, plus other disease problems. Half the troops were sick.[2] It was not uncommon to see men decked out Indian style with only a wrap-around loin cloth. Many had no shoes. Greene noted that the situation was "wretched beyond description."

Of the 2,307 men on roll only 1,482 were present. The rest had evaporated into the countryside or headed home after their enlistments expired. Of those remaining a mere 800 were capable of battle.

## Greene: A Resourceful Leader

Worse yet, the disaster at Camden left the army devoid of wagons, horses, and supplies. Food remained scarce also. The surrounding countryside had been picked clean by the British. So, the entire success of this army would depend on Greene's resourcefulness, a trait he developed while serving as Washington's quartermaster. After taking command, Greene then did the unthinkable: he divided

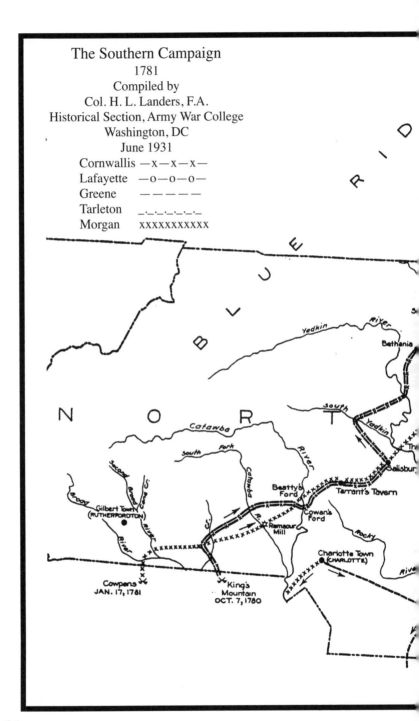

The Southern Campaign
1781
Compiled by
Col. H. L. Landers, F.A.
Historical Section, Army War College
Washington, DC
June 1931
Cornwallis —x—x—x—
Lafayette —o—o—o—
Greene — — — — —
Tarleton _._._._._._
Morgan xxxxxxxxxxx

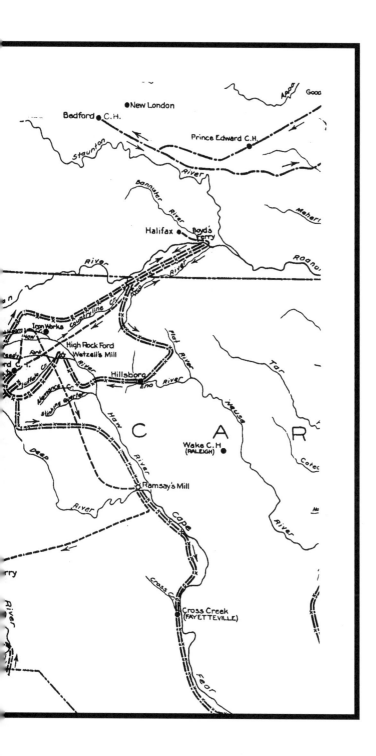

his inferior force into two groups. Brigadier General Daniel Morgan, a battle-hardened frontier Indian fighter, commanded a contingent of Maryland and Delaware continentals along with some militia. They proceeded westward to strike and harass the enemy, and recruit more militia. This strategy offered some protection from Cornwallis as Greene took the rest of his army southeast to Cheraw, South Carolina, to recuperate and get ready to fight.

Nathanael Greene
(National Archives)

Greene rightly guessed that this action would cause Cornwallis to divide his troops in turn. This he did, sending his light corps under Lt. Colonel Banastre Tarleton to push Morgan as hard as possible. "Bloody" Tarleton, his name an epithet for terror and cruelty, received his comeuppance when he attacked the "Old Waggoner" Morgan. On January 17, 1781, Tarleton sent his men headlong into battle and 90 percent were killed, wounded, or captured at the Cowpens.

### *Cornwallis Turns To Revenge*

The incident infuriated Cornwallis, who garnered his reinforcements, and headed after Morgan's troops. British honor had to be restored. Anticipating this revenge, Morgan headed east toward the Catawba River as fast as possible with his British prisoners.

When Morgan's men kept getting farther away, Cornwallis halted his army at Ramsour's Mill, North Carolina, on January 25, 1781. He decided then and there to make an all-out effort to crush the Americans. For three days he stripped down his army to give it mobility. Everything not essential, including wagons, tents, baggage, and any provisions that could not be carried in a knapsack were burned.

Cornwallis burned all his own personal belongings and his officers did likewise. Even the rum supply was poured out. As British General Charles O'Hara later wrote:[3]

> . . . without baggage, necessaries, or provisions of
> any sort for officer or soldier, in the most barren
> inhospitable, unhealthy part of North America,
> opposed the most savage, inveterate, perfidious,
> cruel enemy, with zeal and with bayonets only, it
> was resolved to follow Greene's army to the end of
> the world.

The race was on. There was no turning back.

Right after Morgan crossed the Catawba, winter rains made the river unfordable. This gave him a two-day advantage over Cornwallis, who waited for the flooding to subside. Greene realized Cornwallis' persistent nature would soon put Morgan's men in harm's way. With only a few mounted escorts Greene rode through 120 miles of hostile territory to reach Morgan on the east side of the Catawba.

### *Greene Develops Bold Strategy*

Morgan thought the safety of the army could only be ensured by retreating into the western mountains. But Greene had another strategy in mind. He wanted the troops left at Cheraw, South Carolina, under General Huger's command, to march 125 miles north to Salisbury, North Carolina. Morgan's men would march northeast to unite the armies there on the west side of the Yadkin River. That would draw Cornwallis further away from his base in South Carolina, stretching his supply lines to the limit. Greene also hoped

27

enough local militia would turn out along his line of retreat so that a stand could be made against the British on ground of his own choosing. Advancing northward would also put the American army near reinforcements and supplies in Virginia.

It was a bold and daring initiative, replete with danger. Cornwallis commanded a contingent of the King's Household Guards, a regiment of Hessian mercenary soldiers or Jägers, Tarleton's Legion, and three British regular infantry units, the Royal Welsh Fusiliers, the 33rd Regiment of foot, and the 2nd Battalion of Fraser's Highlanders. These were battle-hardened British troops, and there were more of them—better equipped and better supplied. Greene's longsightedness had perceived the dangers inherent in such a hazardous retreat. He had previously instructed Lt. Colonel Edward Carrington, an able quartermaster, to explore and map the Dan River straddling the Virginia-North Carolina border. Carrington also received orders to gather enough boats to transport the whole force across the river if need be. Greene instructed Edward Stevens, Major General of Virginia Militia, along with General Thaddeus Kosciuszko, a Polish patriot and engineer, to do the same at the Catawba and Yadkin rivers. Flatboats that could be rolled on wheels or carried in wagons were to be collected or built.

### Cornwallis Arrives Too Late

Cornwallis finally crossed the Catawba February 1st. He struggled to catch Morgan's troops heading east to cross the Yadkin, but poor roads, torrential rains, and darkness caused his advanced guard under General O'Hara to come up short. Greene and Morgan crossed the Yadkin during the night of February 2nd on boats gathered for that purpose. The British arrived hours later. A frustrated Cornwallis fitfully bombarded the enemy encampment on the other bank with cannon, but to no avail.

Cornwallis then made a 50-mile northern detour to ford the Yadkin, and march east toward Salem, attempting to cut off the advancing rebels. But the Americans swerved east toward Guilford Courthouse for a preplanned meeting with Huger, who had been redirected there.

After marching 47 miles in 48 hours Greene's exhausted troops reached Guilford on February 7th.[4] General Huger's troops arrived over the next day or so, numbed and drenched by the freezing rains of winter. Many had walked the entire 125 miles barefoot.

Along with Huger's men arrived Light-Horse Harry Lee and his famed Legion. Harry Lee, the father of Confederate General Robert E. Lee, commanded an elite group of continentals composed of cavalry and infantry. Lee's fast moving Legion had specialized in guerrilla warfare in South Carolina while aiding Francis Marion, the Swamp Fox. Resplendent in "plumed helmets, dark green tunics, white breeches, and black boots,"[5] they looked every inch dashing heroes.

Greene's army recombined at Guilford Courthouse. By February 9th Cornwallis' army arrived at Salem, North Carolina, 25 miles to the west of Guilford. Cornwallis was now in position to cut off Greene's escape, since both armies were nearly equidistant from some of the upper fords of the Dan. It was still anybody's race.

### *Greene Holds Council of War*

Also, on February 9th Major General Greene held a council of war.[6] Brigadier Generals Isaac Huger and Daniel Morgan attended, as well as Colonel Otho Williams, who had fought courageously at Camden. Greene noted that the army consisted of 1,426 infantry "badly armed and distressed for want of clothing." A militia force of 600 was also "badly armed." In addition he said, " To all these circumstances is added that of the Army's being now without Provisions and no Magazines of any sort within our reach."

Greene reluctantly concluded his army ought to retreat to the Dan River. The decision weighed heavily upon him. To abandon North Carolina would leave it to the British. This continual retreat could also end in disgrace, because such actions don't win battles. Despite these concerns, the council unanimously agreed to withdraw to the Dan.

The race to the Dan entered a new phase the next day—February 10, 1781. The American Army's objectives on the Dan River lay 70 miles away. Greene divided his army once again. Since Daniel Morgan was sidelined because of illness, General Greene appointed Colonel Otho Williams to command a light corps of 700 men.[7] They were to screen the retreat of the main body and hold off British advance forces.

Greene's main body of troops marched northeasterly away from Cornwallis toward the lower fords of the Dan. Greene's plan was to enter Halifax County, Virginia and cross the river at Irwin's and Boyd's ferries,[8] both located just west of the present town of South Boston. The light troops proceeded northwardly, hoping to deceive Cornwallis about the true direction of Greene's army.

## Deception of Cornwallis Pays Off

Cornwallis took the bait simply because he thought Greene had no choice but to cross the Dan River at the shallower fords to the west. Cornwallis considered the lower fords unavailable due to flooding by winter rains. He didn't suspect that Colonel Carrington had been assembling boats from along the river so that Greene's army could cross the Dan downstream over these swollen waters. Neither did he know that Kosciusko was engaged in building fortifications on the south side of the Dan to protect Greene's crossing.

So much was at stake in this retreat. Light-Horse Harry Lee in his memoirs of the southern campaign expressed the sentiment of the time:[9]

> No operation during the war more attracted the
> public attention than did this; not only the toils and
> dangers encountered by a brave general and his
> brave army interested the sympathy of a nation, but
> the safety of the South, hanging on its issue, excited
> universal concern. The danger of this contingency
> alarmed the hearts of all . . .

Nathanael Greene's lone army stood between the southern colonies and British domination. If Greene's army were to be destroyed by Cornwallis, Georgia and the Carolinas would remain in British hands and Virginia would eventually fall. Lee said "The stoutest heart trembled lest the Potomac should become the boundary of British dominion on the east of the Blue Ridge."[10]

Besides a determined Cornwallis, another threatening factor was something Greene had no control over. The weather had been cantankerous all along, unfit for man or beast. Now, with Cornwallis so close, the harsh winter conditions made the journey to Virginia more perilous.

It couldn't have been worse. The opposing armies engaged in a hellish march through freezing rain and snow. The slushy red clay mud would frost over at night and soften during the "warmer" daytime. This churning concoction of mud and rain mired up wagons, causing frequent breakdowns. Walking was precarious, both horses and men floundering, sinking into the deeply rutted roads with each step.

Light-Horse Harry Lee describes additional hardships:[11]

> The shoes were generally worn out, the body clothes much tattered, and not more than a blanket for four men. Provisions were not to be found in abundance, so swift was our progress. The single meal allowed us was always scanty . . . being bacon and corn meal.

Both armies plodded along. Cornwallis, undeterred by miserable circumstances, pushed his men hard, dogging Colonel Williams light troops which barely stayed ahead. As they marched, Colonel Williams' men separated the two armies, with Cornwallis and Greene on either side almost parallel to each other.

## Constant Vigilance by the Patriots

To keep Cornwallis' vanguard, with Tarleton's cavalry, from maneuvering around Williams' light corps and attacking Greene's army required extreme vigilance. Half of Williams' men patrolled at night while the other half slept. Lee's cavalry had the hazardous duty of bringing up the rear. The task involved frequent skirmishes since the opposing armies were sometimes within musket range of one another.

By the morning of the 13th Colonel Williams' deception had run its course. Tarleton informed Cornwallis that the main body of Greene's army was heading for the lower Dan instead.

After having deceived Cornwallis into following the road to Dix's Ferry, located on the Dan River near present day Danville, Virginia, Williams took a more direct route to Irwin's Ferry, 20 miles to the east. He detailed Lee's Legion to screen his movements. Cornwallis discovered the ruse and surprised Lee's troops, who barely escaped.

As the day of the 13th wore on, rest became a rarity. The light troops, now in between Cornwallis and Greene's troops, were totally exhausted. On that day Williams despaired to Greene in a dispatch stating the cavalry horses "want refreshment exceedingly" and the infantry were "so excessively fatigued that I am confident that I lose men every day."[12] The British were exhausted as well but both armies marched on. Cornwallis pushed his own men, and the Americans, into the night of February 13th.

## A Cause for Celebration

In the early morning hours of the 14th both sides again stopped briefly, then the race continued unabated throughout the night. At 2 p.m. on the 14th Greene sent a dispatch to Colonel Williams. It read "The greater part of our wagons are over and the troops are crossing." At 5:30 p.m. Greene sent another message noting "All our troops are over . . . I am ready to receive you and give you a hearty welcome."[13] A resounding cheer went up from the American light corps, so loud that it was heard by British General O'Hara's vanguard.

On that eventful afternoon a floating armada greeted Greene's troops at water's edge. Among them were boats gathered from along the Dan River in Halifax and Pittsylvania counties. After the main body crossed over, Williams' corps arrived before sunset. They boarded the waiting boats, while Lee's Legion held off the enemy. Afterwards, Lee's infantry crossed. Finally, between 8-9 p.m., Lee's cavalry embarked on the boats while their horses swam alongside reaching the other side safely. Some accounts report that O'Hara's British troops arrived at the river as the last boat went across. Of course they were too late, the race was over.

Every half-clad, starving, frostbitten American soldier who made it to the Dan that day was a hero. Subordinate officers served with distinction, but Major General Nathanael Greene was the man of the hour. He enjoyed high praise from friend and foe. George Washington wrote Greene, "You may be assured that your retreat before Lord Cornwallis is highly applauded by all ranks, and it reflects much honor upon your military abilities.[14] "Bloody" Tarleton noted in his history of the campaign, "Every measure of the Americans, during the march from Catawba to Virginia, was judiciously designed and vigorously executed."[15] Ten years after the event Otho Williams wrote to Light-Horse Harry Lee, "The retreat of the southern army to Dan River, though now forgotten, was, in my estimation, one of the most masterly and fortunate manoeuvres of our beloved Greene."[16] Others had their own way of looking at this retreat. A tune of that day sung to "Yankee Doodle" goes:

> Cornwallis led a country dance,
> The like was never seen, sir,
> Much retrograde and much advance
> And all with General Greene, sir.
>
> They rambled up and rambled down,
> Joined hands and off they ran, sir,
> And General Greene was like to drown
> Cornwallis in the Dan, sir.

Greene took little time to revel in his escape. He wrote a lengthy report to Washington dated 15 February 1781 at Camp Irwin's Ferry on the Dan River, Virginia. Excerpts from this dispatch are poignant reminders of the courageous effort of Greene's army in the Race to the Dan:[17]

> The miserable situation of the troops for want of clothing had rendered the march the most painful imaginable, several hundreds of the soldiers tracking the ground with their bloody feet . . . Our Army are in good spirits notwith-standing their suffering  and excessive fatigue.

Good spirits indeed! They had marched over 200 miles, the last 40 in 16 hours. Now was a time of relief and a cause for joy. Lee in his *Memoirs* records, "The people of Halifax County received us with the affection of brothers mingled with the admiration of the brave devotion to country just exhibited . . ." The army also enjoyed "wholesome and abundant supplies of food in the rich and friendly county of Halifax."[18] Neighboring Pittsylvania sent aid as well. Help came from all over Southside Virginia. Militia units poured in and also fresh continental troops arrived.

### *Retreat Brought Cornwallis Closer to Defeat*

Meanwhile, all Cornwallis could do was watch. His exhausted British army could go no more. After collecting provisions, the British retreated from the Dan River on February 17th, and marched to Hillsborough, North Carolina. Greene's army followed and engaged Cornwallis at Guilford Courthouse March 15th. Even though Cornwallis' troops held the field, they were mauled so severely that they retreated to Wilmington. From there they ventured to Yorktown, where their world turned upside down.

The importance of the Race to the Dan in rescuing the revolution brings to mind the words of Napoleon, "Every great event hangs by a thread."[19] In February 1781 the serpentine Dan River as it arched into Virginia became such a thread as the American colonies fought for life, liberty, and the pursuit of happiness.

# Endnotes

1. Burke Davis. *The Campaign That Won America: The Story of Yorktown*. Acorn Press, Eastern National Monument Association, 1970, 93.

2. Thomas E. Baker. *Another Such Victory.* Eastern Acorn Press, Eastern National Park and Monument Association, 1981, 17-18.

3. Comment by Brig. General Charles O'Hara to Duke of Grafton, April 20, 1781.

4. Mark Boatner. *Encyclopedia of The American Revolution.* New York: David McKay Company, 1966, 1023. Boatner adopts the dates of Light-Horse Harry Lee in his memoirs, considering him the most reliable.

5. Noel B. Gerson. *Light-Horse Harry.* New York: Ballantine Books, 1966, 92.

6. Richard K. Showman, Gen Ed. *The Papers of General Nathanael Greene*, Vol. 7, Dec. 1780-Mar. 1781, Chapel Hill, NC: UNC Press, 1994, 261-262.

7. This included 280 infantry under Lt. Col. John E. Howard, 240 dragoons under Lt. Cols. William E. Washington and Henry Lee, 60 Virginia Riflemen, and Lee's infantry. Source: Charles E. Hatch, Jr. *The Battle of Guilford Courthouse*. Washington, DC: National Park Service, July 1971, 2.

8. James M. Owens. "The Site of The First Eventful Failure of Cornwallis," *The Virginia Magazine of History and Biography* 44. January 1936, 211.

9. Henry Lee. *Memoirs of The War in The Southern Department of The United States,* 2 vols. Philadelphia: 1812, 293.

10. Ibid., 294.

11. Ibid., 295.

12. Greene Papers, 285.

13. See Greene Papers, 287 and 302. Also Boatner, 1026. Also, Lee's *Memoirs*, 291-292. These conflicting references illustrate why historians continue to disagree over the actual date Greene crossed the Dan River.

14. Spurgeon Compton and W. Carroll Headspeth. T*he Retreat To The Dan*. South Boston, VA: *South Boston News*, 1974, 8.

15. Banastre Tarleton. *A History of The Campaigns of 1780 and 1781 in the Southern Province of America*. 1787 Reprint. Spartanburg, SC: Reprint Book Co., 1967, 229.

16. Henry Lee. *The Campaign of 1780-1781 in The Carolinas with Remarks Historical and Critical on Johnson's Life of Greene*. Reprint, Spartanburg, SC: Reprint Book Co., 1975, 125-126.

17. Greene Papers, 293.

18. Francis Hallam Hurt. *An Intimate History of the American Revolution in Pittsylvania County, VA*. Danville, VA: Womack Press, 1976, 129.

19. J. Christopher Herold. *The Age of Napoleon*. New York: American Heritage Library, 1963, 85.

# Biographies of
# British and American Commanders

The following information was gathered from *Appleton's Cyclopedia of American Biography*, by Wilson and Fiske, six volumes, 1887-1889; Lossing's *Pictorial Field-Book of the Revolution*, and other sources.

### Lord Cornwallis

Lord Cornwallis was born in 1737 and on the death of his father in 1762 became Earl Cornwallis, also inheriting his father's seat in the House of Lords. "On the American question his sympathies were strongly with the American colonists, and in the famous debate on the repeal of the Stamp Act he was signalized as one of the five peers who voted in favor of unconditional repeal, accompanied by the explicit renunciation of the right of taxing America."

British General Lord Cornwallis
(National Archives)

Early in his military career he became known for the personal valor and skill with which he handled his regiment. In 1761 he was promoted to Lt. Colonel, then later to General. "As a military commander [during the Revolution] he was bold and vigilant though unable to cope with the transcendent talents of Washington and Greene."

After the Revolution he returned to England, where he served with distinction in other government posts. In 1786, as a field marshal, he was appointed Governor General of India and commander-in-chief of British forces there. When he returned to England in 1794, he became master of ordinance with a seat in the cabinet. Later he was appointed Lord Lieutenant of Ireland, and afterwards was sent again to India where he died in Benares in 1805.

### *Banastre Tarleton*

Banastre Tarleton was born in Liverpool, England in 1754 and received education as a lawyer. He joined Cornwallis when he came to America and served as Lt. Colonel organizing "Tarleton's Legion," which was composed of light infantry and cavalry with a few field pieces. His forces could move faster than the regular army and became effective in partisan warfare in the Southern Campaign.

Banastre Tarleton
From original by Sir Joshua Reynolds, 1782

Known for refusing quarter to surrendering men, he became identified by the epithet "Bloody Tarleton" since his tactics involved butchery of the enemy. However, his forces were nearly destroyed by Daniel Morgan's brilliant tactical maneuvers at the Cowpens.

Toward the end of the Revolution, Tarleton's forces barely missed capturing Thomas Jefferson at Monticello. After Cornwallis' surrender at Yorktown, Tarleton returned to England, where he was promoted to full colonel, then elected to parliament from Liverpool in 1790. He attained the rank of full general in 1812, became a baronet in 1815 and was knighted in 1820. He died in 1833.

## Charles O'Hara

Charles O'Hara was born in 1730, and entered the army in 1756, and later became a captain in the Coldstream Guards. He came to the Colonies in 1780 with his regiment and served under Cornwallis as Brigadier General, commanding the vanguard in the pursuit of General Morgan after the Battle of Cowpens in 1781. O'Hara also led the left wing of Cornwallis' army at Guilford Courthouse, where he was severely wounded. "He [Charles O'Hara] was a brave and enterprising soldier and a strict disciplinarian."

At the surrender in Yorktown, General O'Hara was designated by Cornwallis to surrender his sword; however, General Washington refused to accept it and insisted that O'Hara present it to General Benjamin Lincoln instead. Lincoln had commanded the 5,500 troops that were forced to surrender to the British in Charleston, South Carolina when Cornwallis initiated his southern invasion.

After the war, O'Hara served several British colonies as governor and finally became Governor of Gibraltar in 1797. He was promoted to major general and died there in 1802.

## Nathanael Greene

Nathanael Greene was born in Rhode Island in 1742, the fourth child in a family of nine. He grew up working in the family ironworks, while diligently studying Latin, geometry, and Euclid plus other literary writings. He was later elected to the Rhode Island legislature. Greene was an outspoken opponent of the British in their disputes with the Colonies and began to study military science, convinced that the Colonies and Britain would eventfully be at war with one another.

In 1774, after failing to be elected company lieutenant, he entered the newly formed Kentish Guards as a private. Even that position was in jeopardy, however, due to the slight limp in Greene's walk. Yet, after the Battle of Bunker Hill, the Rhode Island Assembly raised three regiments of troops to join the forces around Boston and appointed Greene as Brigadier General.

Nathanael Greene
*A History of the United States*, 1886

During the Revolution, General Greene engaged Cornwallis in November 1776 and helped prevent him from capturing the American army during its retreat across the Hudson River. Greene also commanded the left wing of Washington's army in the dramatic capture of Hessian soldiers in the Battle of Trenton on December 25, 1776. At Brandywine, General Greene again foiled an attempt by Cornwallis to rout the American army under Washington. He also successfully covered the retreat of Anthony Wayne's forces in the Battle of Germantown.

Washington appointed General Greene as Quartermaster General in 1778, a position he held until he assumed command of West Point in 1780. His claim to fame, however, was the restoration of the Southern army and its eventual success in reaching Virginia ahead of Cornwallis. Reinforcements allowed Greene to deliver a devastating blow to Cornwallis at Guilford Courthouse, a bloody battle which signaled the end of the Revolutionary War.

After Guilford Courthouse, Greene's forces recaptured all the back country of South Carolina and Georgia. In 1781, after an engagement at Eutaw Springs, Greene marched in triumph with his army to Charleston, South Carolina.

He returned to Rhode Island after the war but in 1785 moved to a plantation at Mulberry Grove in Georgia, which that state had presented to him in honor of his military service. It was there on June 19, 1786, while walking outside, that he suffered a sun stroke and died at age 44. He was survived by his wife Catherine and five children. He is buried in Savannah.

*Appleton's Cyclopedia* adds this conclusion: "His series of campaigns from December 1780 to September 1781 will be a comparison to the best work of Turenne or Washington. What he might have done on a greater scale and with more ample resources, it is, of course, impossible to say; but the intellectual qualities that he showed were precisely those that have won distinction from the foremost strategists of modern times. It would be difficult to praise too highly the superb manoeuvring that drew Cornwallis 200 miles from his base, force a battle on him at Guilford under such circumstances that victory proved hardly less fatal to him than defeat, and thus turned him off into Virginia, leaving Greene's hands free to drive Rawdon from Camden and reconquer South Carolina."

There are monuments to Greene in Washington, DC and Savannah, as well as an equestrian statue at The Guilford Courthouse National Military Park in Greensboro, North Carolina. The memorial is remarkable in its appeal and portrays Greene as the confident and dashing military leader that he was.

### Henry "Light-Horse" Lee III

"Light-Horse Harry" Lee, or by his given name, Henry Lee III, was born 1756 near Dumfries, Virginia. He was graduated from Princeton College in 1773, and when the Revolution began he was commissioned a captain in the Virginia Light Dragoons. Lee conducted lightening raids on enemy supply trains and, in a surprise attack at Paulus Hook, New Jersey, he captured 400 British soldiers while losing only one man. His superb horsemanship during that enterprise won him accolades as a natural cavalryman and earned him the

"Light-Horse Harry" Lee

nickname "Light-Horse Harry." For this outstanding exploit, Congress voted him a gold medal, the only one given to any American officer below the rank of general during the entire Revolutionary War.

After his promotion to Lieutenant Colonel he was sent to the Southern Department of the army, serving especially under General Greene where Lee's Legion, as his dragoons were called, did exceptional service as part of the rear guard in the Race to the Dan. Lee's service was invaluable also at Guilford Courthouse and Eutaw Springs. After the surrender at Yorktown, he left the army because of ill health.

From 1789-1791 he served in Virginia's House of Delegates and was Governor of Virginia from 1791-1794. In 1794 Washington sent him to suppress the Whiskey Rebellion in Pennsylvania. He was a major general from 1798-1800 and served in the United States Congress from 1799-1801.

When George Washington died, Congress asked Light-Horse Harry Lee to deliver a tribute. He coined this famous phrase which he included in his eulogy for Washington at the funeral: "First in war, first in peace, and first in the hearts of his countrymen . . ."

After the death of Washington, Lee's support of his six-member family, plus his ruinous land speculations, reduced him to poverty. He spent a year in debtor's prison when his son Civil War General Robert E. Lee was two years old. While there in his 12- by 5-foot cell Lee wrote his *Memoirs of the War in the Southern Department of the United States*, still a classic text about the Southern Campaign during the Revolution.

His last years were filled with ill heath and continued impoverishment. He sought out the climate of the West Indies as a remedy for his poor health but to no avail. When he attempted to return home, Harry Lee spent his last money on a ship ticket in February 1818 to get to Alexandria, Virginia. But due to his poor physical condition, he asked the ship's captain to put him off at the Cumberland Island, Georgia, home of Nathanael Greene. When he arrived, he could neither walk by himself or ride a horse, so two sailors carried him ashore. When Greene's wife and children greeted him on this unexpected visit, Lee was derelict in his appearance, wearing the now threadbare clothes he had worn when he initially came to the Caribbean from Virginia—he had not been able to afford more. Yet, they welcomed him as a hero, and when he died in March 1818, he was given a full military funeral and buried beside Nathanael Greene. No relatives attended and no immediate family members came or even visited the grave of this hero of the Revolution until his son General Robert E. Lee visited the cemetery in 1862. It is said that he placed a wreath upon his father's grave and silently wept.

## *Daniel Morgan*

Daniel Morgan was born about 1736 of Welsh ancestry. His military career began as a teamster in British General Braddock's army. He fought in the French and Indian War where he engaged in a fierce battle with Indians being wounded for the only time in his life. He was later commissioned a captain of militia in Frederick County, Virginia and fought in Lord Dunmore's War.

In 1775 he became captain of a Virginia company of riflemen that assisted in the Siege of Boston. He served throughout the Revolution in various capacities under Generals Benedict Arnold, Washington, Gates, and lastly as a Brigadier General with Nathanael Greene. He is most

Daniel Morgan
Painting by Chappell, Johnson E. Fry Publ., 1861

43

remembered as the Hero of Cowpens, where his defeat of Tarleton's cavalry severely disrupted Cornwallis' plans to quickly destroy another American army. "In point of tactics it was the most brilliant battle of the Revolutionary War."

Morgan was elected to Congress in 1796 and retired to his home in Winchester, Virginia,, before the end of his term due to ill health. He died there in 1802.

## *Otho Holland Williams*

Otho Williams
Lossing's *Pictorial Field-Book,* 1852

Otho Holland Williams was of Welsh ancestry, born in Maryland in 1749, and orphaned at twelve years old. During the Revolution he was wounded and imprisoned by the British. Upon his exchange he was appointed colonel in command of the 6th Maryland Regiment. He later served as adjutant general in the southern army under General Gates and lastly under General Greene.

Williams' light corps distinguished itself as a rear guard during Greene's race to the Dan River. Near the close of the war he was appointed brigadier general. Afterwards he returned to Baltimore where the governor appointed him collector of the port, a position he served until his death around 1800.

## *William Washington*

William Washington was a distant cousin of George Washington, born in Stafford County, Virginia, in 1752. During the Revolution he fought at Brooklyn, Long Island, Trenton, and Princeton. In 1779 he commanded a light corps in Lincoln's army at Charleston and later, as part of Morgan's forces, fought bravely at the Cowpens where Tarleton's forces were soundly defeated. Congress awarded Washington a silver medal for his effort in that battle. During that battle

Washington engaged in a personal encounter with Tarleton, wounding the celebrated British cavalry leader.

Lossing reports the following story relating to this incident in his *Pictorial Field-Book of the Revolution*. When Tarleton was in Halifax County, North Carolina, on his way to Virginia near the war's end, he was at the house of an American woman, Mrs. Wilie Jones. He spoke sarcastically to her about Colonel Washington, saying he was illiterate and hardly able to write his name. The woman responded, "Colonel, you ought to know better, for you bear on your person proof that he knows very well how to make his mark!"

William Washington
From Engraving of Peale Portrait
by J. B. Forrest, 1819

Washington fought bravely at Guilford Courthouse, at Hobkirk's Hill and also at Eutaw Springs, where he had his horse shot out from under him and became a British prisoner until the close of the war. He married in South Carolina and settled in Charleston, representing that district in the Legislature.

When President Adams appointed George Washington Commander-in-Chief of the American army, William Washington joined General Washington's staff as a brigadier general. He died in 1810.

### John Eager Howard

John Eager Howard was born in Baltimore County, Maryland,, in 1752 into a wealthy family. He joined the army at the onset of the American Revolution and served in various battles including Germantown and Monmouth as an officer in the 4th Maryland Regiment. In 1780 as Lieutenant Colonel in the 5th Maryland Regiment, he fought at Camden, South Carolina,, with General Gates and then served under Nathanael Greene.

John E. Howard
*Lossing's Pictorial Field-Book*, 1852

At the Cowpens, his Maryland regiment attacked the British in a bayonet charge that ensured the victory. Afterward, Congress awarded him a silver medal for his heroic efforts. He had displayed great gallantry; at one time he held the swords of seven British officers who had surrendered to him.

Howard commanded the light infantry in Otho Holland Williams' corps during Greene's retreat across the Dan River. He also fought at Guilford Courthouse and later at Hobkirk's Hill and Eutaw Springs. There his command was reduced to 30 men and he the only surviving officer. He ordered a final charge and was severely wounded.

After the war, Colonel Howard served as Governor of Maryland from 1789-1792 and in the United States Senate from 1796-1803. In 1816 he was a candidate for vice-president. He died in Maryland in 1827.

### Thaddeus Kosciusko

Thaddeus Kosciusko was a Polish patriot born in Lithuania in 1746. He studied at the military academy of Warsaw, continued his education in France, then joined the army of Poland attaining the rank of captain. He left Poland after an unrequited love affair with the daughter of the Marquis of Lithuania and came to America to assist in the Revolution. When presented to General Washington, Kosciusko said, "I came to America to fight as a volunteer for American Independence." Washington asked, "What can you do?" Kosciusko's response was, "Try me."

He received a commission as colonel of engineers, served under General Gates and planned the encampment and post of Gates' army

Thaddeus Kosciusko
1783 engraving, *Memoirs of Kusciusko*

at Saratoga. His fortifications were so well done that British General Burgoyne found it impossible to dislodge the Americans. Kosciusko later became adjutant to General Washington. He was chiefly responsible for the fortifications at West Point and in 1828 the corps of cadets erected a monument to him. In the Southern Campaign of 1780-1781 he served with distinction in General Greene's Army.

At the end of the American Revolution, Kosciusko returned to Poland and was appointed major general. His forces distinguished themselves against the Russian army on several occasions and his countrymen later invested him as dictator and general-in-chief. In 1794 he raised a peasant army of 5,000 armed only with scythes. He was covered with wounds in battle and imprisoned at St. Petersburg, Russia. After the death of Catherine the Great, he was released.

He visited the United States again in 1797 and was honored with a land grant from Congress. Kosciusko eventually moved to Switzerland where he died by a fall from his horse over a cliff. He was buried at the Cathedral of Cracow. At his grave a mound of dirt rose 150 feet high, brought from every battlefield of Poland.

### *Edward Carrington*
Edward Carrington was born in Cumberland County, Virginia,, in 1749. At the outbreak of the American Revolution he was commissioned Lieutenant Colonel of artillery. He was detached to the South and became a British prisoner at Charleston, then served General

Edward Carrington
Library of Congress

Gates, and later became Quartermaster General to Nathanael Greene.

Carrington explored the Dan River and made preparations for Greene's army to cross on boats at Boyd's and Irwin's ferries near South Boston, Virginia. He commanded artillery at Hobkirk's Hill in April 1781 and also at Yorktown. After the war he was a delegate from Virginia to the Continental Congress in 1785-86. Colonel Carrington also served as jury foreman in Aaron Burr's trial for treason in 1807. Edward Carrington died in Richmond, Virginia, in 1810.

## *Isaac Huger*

Born in 1742 on the Santee River in South Carolina, Isaac Huger grew up on a large plantation. He represented his native state in the First Continental Congress, later rising through the ranks and becoming a Brigadier General in the Southern army. He assisted in defending Georgia during the British invasion and was wounded at the Battle of Stono during the Siege of Charleston in 1780.

Isaac Huger

He served with General Nathanael Greene during the Race to the Dan, marching his troops from Cheraw, South Carolina, to Guilford then to the Dan River. He was wounded again in the Battle of Guilford Courthouse but later fought in the Battle of Hobkirk's Hill. In 1782 he was elected to the South Carolina General Assembly and in 1789 was appointed by President Washington as the first U.S. Marshall of South Carolina. General Huger died in 1797 at the age of 54.

# Greene's Crossing of the Dan: How Important Was It?

The crossing of the Dan River on February 13-14, 1781, by General Nathanael Greene's army came at the end of a retreat across the Carolinas during a second British attempt to invade the Southern Colonies. The last four days of that retreat became a heated race with Lord Cornwallis' British army, in which both British and American forces were in constant contact. Finally, in boats gathered at the Dan River near South Boston, Virginia, Greene's army escaped across the rain-swollen stream. Sometime later the vanguard of Cornwallis' army appeared on the other side. Cornwallis, stranded without boats and the inability to ford the fast moving and engorged river, saw no alternative but to retreat.

What General Greene had accomplished was nothing less than heroic. At the end of the 230-mile march achieved under the worst of circumstances, General Greene had not only saved his army, but in doing so had rescued the American Revolution from certain disaster.

Of course, there were other crucial moments when the Revolution was saved even before Greene's crossing of the Dan River. The victories at Trenton and Sarasota, the resurgence of the American army after Valley Forge, the Battle of Cowpens and King's Mountain, and the arrival of French ships off the coast near Yorktown prior to Cornwallis' capitulation, all played monumental roles in continuing the momentum of the Patriot cause. However, by the time of the Race to the Dan, American independence had still not been won; in fact, it appeared more hopeless than ever. But after the Race to the Dan, events and circumstances caused the British to lose the success that they had enjoyed in the South. Thus the Race to the Dan had a domino effect that forced all subsequent events toward Yorktown. Said another way, if Yorktown can be likened to a pendulum weight, the crossing of the Dan River was the string upon which it moved.

Though sometimes neglected in historical writings about the Revolutionary War, the crossing of the Dan River by Nathanael Greene's army determined the remainder of the course of that war, especially the reconquering of the South, and Cornwallis' eventual surrender.

James Owen in an article for the *Virginia Magazine of History and Biography* in 1936 wrote, "Modern students of American history have shown a strange lack of appreciation of the vital relationship existing between the destiny of the United States and the campaign which culminated in the crossing of the Dan River" (211-212).

To understand the magnitude of Greene's achievement and why his retreat before Cornwallis receives little credit for its pivotal role in the American Revolution is the subject of this essay. In order to do so, we must first look at events in the Northern and Middle Colonies prior to and during the time of the Southern campaign.

## *Stalemate in the North*

Revolutionary war history is awash with images and stories of the Boston Massacre, the Boston Tea Party, Paul Revere's Ride and the battles of Lexington and Concord and Bunker Hill. Though these events were instrumental in pushing the Colonies toward independence, they were not decisive. After the Declaration of Independence in July 1776, the British focused their attention on New York. Yet, by December of that year, Washington's army had lost New York—with strategic sites including Forts Washington and Lee in British hands. Washington's 3,000 men were in full retreat as Cornwallis crossed the Hudson River with 8,000 men and pursued the American Army through New Jersey. Washington's army was finally forced across the Delaware River into Pennsylvania, but on Christmas day in December 1776, in a daring move, Washington recrossed the Delaware and captured a significant Hessian force at Trenton. The feat boosted morale in the American Colonies, even though it did not greatly reduce the British threat.

Washington had showed his mettle at the Battle of Trenton and later at Princeton, but by September 1777 he was still bogged down in and around New Jersey. Although the British surrendered General Burgoyne's army at Saratoga, about the same time that month the British captured the new American capitol at Philadelphia on September 21st, sending the Congress scurrying. By June 1778, the British decided to leave Philadelphia, which was not a strategic location anyway, and return to New York. A French fleet attempted to intercept the British but arrived too late to engage Clinton's British Army. While on the march, British forces were confronted at Monmouth by a better supplied and more disciplined American army fresh from Valley Forge. That battle was indecisive, but it showed that the American rebels could hold their own against veteran British troops.

The rest of the summer of 1778 held dashed hopes. Not only did the French fail to take on the British before they left Philadelphia, but they also failed to attack them afterward at New York because the French fleet could not enter the harbor. Later, those same French forces, along with Americans, failed to recapture Newport, Rhode Island, from the British.

In the beginning the British envisioned a rapid end to the war with the summary defeat of the upstart rebels who dared oppose the military might of the British Empire. The British were denied such a quick victory because the American spirit was stronger than British cold steel. At the end of 1778, with the war at a standstill, British troops controlled New York; Washington's army, though barely surviving, was still around—camped out in New Jersey.

The survival of Washington's army had prevented the total collapse of the American Revolution. Winston Churchill in his *History of the English Speaking People* wrote, "Simply to have kept his army in existence during these years was probably Washington's greatest contribution to the Patriot cause" (204). Washington had done what on the American side clearly showed his genius, but during the years 1778 to 1780 the army remained in the field but continued to flounder. Who would have predicted that that army would survive to accept the surrender of a Bristish Army in 1781?

Although success was infrequent, all the events of the Northern Campaign were important and not to be minimized. They had their place politically and militarily in wearing down British resolve and wresting the Colonies free of British domination. Yet, neither Trenton nor Saratoga nor other challenges in the North to the British army brought an end to the Revolution. Those events did, however, have a cumulative effect in setting the stage for the Southern Campaign, during which the Revolution was eventually won.

## *British Invade the Southern Colonies*

As the stalemate continued, the British considered a new strategy—a Southern campaign. This was influenced of course by the French entrance into the war after the Americans defeated Burgoyne's army at Saratoga. But there was also another more important reason. Hugh Rankin in *Rebels and Redcoats* wrote:

> The inherent military weakness of these thinly
> populated states, their remoteness from the North
> and its protection, and the undispelled illusion of
> sleeping Tory power in the backcountry, constantly
> drew the thoughts of the King, like a compass
> needle, to the possibility of back door warfare
> against Washington's army (448).

On December 29, 1778, British forces captured Savannah, Georgia, after the American commander Major General Robert Howe offered a poor defense of the city. A later attempt to free the city by French and American forces under General Benjamin Lincoln failed. Thereafter, all of Georgia was subjugated as the British continued their advances. In *Rebels and Redcoats* the authors conclude:

> The failure of the allies [French and Americans] to
> oust the British from Georgia was nothing short of
> calamitous for the rebellion. A victory at Savannah
> would have deprived [British General] Clinton of a
> base from which to invade the rest of the South, and
> the whole plan of the King for reducing the colonies
> one by one, working northward would have gone

awry. With the war stalemated in the North, the
British loss of a foothold in the South would have
shortened the war immeasurably (455).

Failure by the French and Americans to recapture Savannah gave the
British confidence that a Southern invasion would be effective, so
General Clinton, Commander-in-Chief of British forces in America
and his subordinate Cornwallis sailed South with the intentions of
invading Charleston and marching through the Carolinas.

Meanwhile, in May 1779, Washington's own words in a letter to his
brother Jack described his desperation at the situation at hand in the
North:

> [It is] my opinion that the enemy will strain every
> nerve to push the war with vigor this campaign . . .
> By a bill which passed both Houses of Parliament
> every parish in the Kingdom is called upon to
> furnish two Men. These it is said will be immedi-
> ately had, & will amount in the whole to 27,000
> recruits for their army . . . In a word, our conduct has
> been the very reverse of the enemy's, for while they
> are doing everything to prepare vigorously for the
> campaign now opening, we were doing nothing —
> nay, worse than nothing . . . [I] lament, which I do
> most pathetically that decay of public virtue with
> which people were inspired at the beginning of the
> contest.

A few lines later Washington despairs further, stating, " I am very
apprehensive for the fate of Charlestown" (Andrist, 192-193).

That winter Washington's troops wintered in Morristown, New
Jersey. There he wrote a desperate letter to Congress and the Governors of Maryland, Delaware, New York, New Jersey, and Pennsylvania. His letter dated December 16, 1779, reads in part,

> The situation of the Army with respect to supplies is
> beyond description alarming . . . Our magazines are

absolutely empty every where and our commissaries entirely destitute of Money or Credit to replenish them . . . Unless some extraordinary and immediate exertions are made by the States, from which we draw our supplies, there is every appearance that the Army will infallibly disband in a fortnight (Andrist, 194).

Despite Washington's plea, the situation only worsened. The day before Christmas Washington ordered corn intended for the horses to be ground up and given to the men. By May 1780 Connecticut troops in the Army mutinied. They had had no meat in ten days and no pay in five months. "The Army was melting away with the state governments doing little about replacement recruiting" (Andrist, 196).

As the situation with the army deteriorated  Washington received even more bad news confirming what he had worried about earlier: Charlestown (Charleston) had been captured on May 12 along with the bulk of the American army in the South. American General Benjamin Lincoln surrendered his entire army of 5,500 troops. That event emboldened the Loyalists and encouraged more civil war in the South. Conflicts escalated between partisan groups of Loyalists and Rebels as members of communities squared off against one another.

As the Southern Campaign continued to unfold in August 1780, the American army in the North still had almost no food and gained less than half of the troops requested from the states. The army had to scavenge the countryside for provisions. This meant the distasteful task of taking food from local inhabitants, who earlier had endured the same treatment from British troops. In a letter dated August 27, 1780, Washington wrote that his army had had to ". . . assume the odious character of the plunderers, instead of the protectors of the people, the direct consequence of which must be to alienate their minds from the army, and insensibly from the cause" (Andrist, 198). Once again Washington related that he didn't see how the army could remain together much longer unless circumstances changed quickly.

Not only was the cause of American independence at a breaking point in the North, in mid-August 1780 Cornwallis had handed a second American army under General Horatio Gates a devastating defeat at Camden, South Carolina. Wagons, supplies—nearly everything—was lost in this ignominious defeat. After throwing down their weapons, the militia evaporated into the countryside. The American continentals fought bravely but were overwhelmed by the British. Gates shamefully outran his own troops 180 miles to Hillsborough, North Carolina.

The news from the North and the South now essentially paralleled one another. Washington's army was barely holding on, but luckily the British, crippled by war with both France and Spain, had to guard their holdings around the world, especially the West Indies, against attack. They were stretched to commit more troops to the American colonies. In fact, there was dissension in England over this pro-tracted war and fear of an invasion of the British Isles itself by a combined French and Spanish fleet. So more troops were not forthcoming to mount a Northern offensive against Washington. Yet, Washington and his army and the Northern Colonies themselves were not operating from a position of strength and were not able to dislodge the British.

The help of the French had previously consisted of supplies and arms but not troops due to the need for the French fleet in the West Indies. Every attempt by the French fleet to assist the American cause was unsuccessful to the point that some colonists lost faith in the French commitment.

The situation among the American Colonies was beyond desperate; the Congress was broke, food was scarce, and recruiting for Washington's army was harder than ever. With Washington's army teetering on the verge of collapse on any given day, and three major defeats of the Southern army at Savannah, Charleston and Camden, one would think that another such blow might have proved fatal.

It easily could have. It was bad enough that Howe had relinquished Savannah, or that Lincoln failed to take the initiative and lost

Charleston, or that Gates' leadership proved pathetic at Camden, but in September 1780 Benedict Arnold, another American general, turned traitor and nearly handed over the strategic Northern fortress of West Point to the British.

The effect of this traitorous plot cannot be underestimated. Had it been successful the war's momentum might have turned in favor of the British. Winston Churchill wrote in *The Age of Revolution* that:

> Arnold's act of betrayal, though discovered in time, had a marked, if temporary, effect on the sentiment and cohesion of the Patriots. They had been very near disaster. Many Americans were strongly opposed to the war, and Loyalists throughout the country either openly or secretly supported the British. The South was already smitten with hideous civil strife in which American slew American and each man suspected his neighbor. Was the same frightful process to engulf the North, hitherto steadfast in the Patriot cause? If the commander of West Point was a traitor, then who could be trusted? (206).

Arnold's betrayal had brought low morale even lower and the almost uncontested superiority of the British in the South now made the Revolutionary War situation truly grave. General Clinton, confident the British Southern campaign's goals could be accomplished, left for the North with several thousand British troops. Cornwallis was consigned to mop up, in what seemed easy pickings so far. The successful invasions of Georgia and South Carolina had created what appeared to be an open road to Virginia and the British juggernaut seemed unstoppable.

After establishing armed British outposts across South Carolina, Cornwallis prepared to advance into North Carolina. However, continual harassment of his army by partisan groups plus one significant American victory stood in his way. A breakthrough finally came for the Patriot cause on October 7, 1780, when a disastrous blow to Cornwallis' army gave the American Colonies a ray of hope about the outcome of the Southern campaign. The left flank of the British army was defeated at King's Mountain by frontier militias, referred to as overmountain men mostly from country west of the Appalachians.

The Battle of King's Mountain slowed Cornwallis down, and he retreated to Winnsborough, South Carolina. There he waited for reinforcements from General Leslie, who was initially directed to land in Virginia at the Chesapeake Bay. From the Chesapeake Leslie had hoped to advance toward Cornwallis and meet up with him as Cornwallis and his troops advanced northward through the Carolinas. With the change of plans due to the British defeat at King's Mountain, Cornwallis' army was substantially reinforced by Leslie's troops. Together they were sure to march toward Virginia and complete the British strategy to subdue the South.

## *Greene's Southern Campaign*

Despite continual harassment by partisan groups, the British army appeared capable of withstanding any challenge. It was an extremely critical time in our young nation's history. But then came Nathanael Greene, chosen by Washington and approved by Congress to head what was left of the Southern Army. He had previously been Washington's Quartermaster and had been by his side through major battles in New York, in New Jersey at Trenton and Princeton, in Philadelphia at Brandywine, Germantown, and Valley Forge, and in New Jersey again at Monmouth. As Washington's designated successor, Nathanael Greene had the Commander-in-Chief's confidence.

No appointment during the American revolution was more timely and critical than this one. Under Greene's leadership, the entire Southern situation changed, though no one would have predicted it at the time. George Washington wrote to Congress upon Greene's appointment noting, "In the command he is going into he will have every disadvantage to struggle with." General Washington noted that if something wasn't done to strengthen the Southern army then, "The history of this war is the history of false hopes" (Rankin, 4). Washington knew the stakes were high. If the remaining American army was lost so would the South be also, and the war itself.

General Greene himself was not totally confident that he could pull off the miracle that a desperate nation needed. He was despondent over what he had heard about the Southern army and thought that the soldiers were "totally unfit for any type of service" (Rankin, 5). He wrote to Washington that, " My only consolation is, that if I fail, I hope it will not be accompanied by any marks of personal disgrace. Censure and reproach will ever follow the unfortunate. This I expect, if I don't succeed . . ." (Rankin, 7).

Even before he assumed command, Greene had agonized over the situation with the remains of Gates' army near Charlotte. After nine days in Philadelphia pleading with Congress for help, Greene came away with good wishes but empty handed. Despite their willingness, the Congress had nothing to offer. Greene met with the governors of other states as he traveled on the way to South Carolina. The results were almost the same. After taking command on December 2, 1780, Greene wrote a lengthy letter to Alexander Hamilton on January 10, 1781, describing his previous efforts to secure supplies.

> At Philadelphia and all my journey through the
> Country, I endeavored to impress upon those in
> power the necessity of sending cloathing and sup-
> plies of every kind immediately to this Army. But
> poverty was urged as a plea or bar to every applica-
> tion. They all promised fair; but I fear will do but
> little: ability is wanting in some and inclination in
> others. Public credit is so totally lost, that private
> people will not give their aid, though they see
> themselves involved in one common ruin (NG
> Papers, 7: 88).

He arrived to take command with no realistic hope of assistance. What he had was all he had and that wasn't much. Greene's experience as Washington's Quartermaster and his own initiative developed as a field commander would have to be enough.

The troops themselves were, as Greene described them, "nothing but the shadow of an army in the midst of distress." Food was scarce, supplies and wagons were few, and clothes were in short supply as well. He had no money and later had to pay seamstresses in Salisbury with salt to make apparel of coarse cloth for his troops. Out of 2,307 troops on roll, over half were militia, and only 800 were equipped and ready to fight. There was extreme sickness and hunger.

The Southern army had also become a ragged undisciplined mob. Militia units plundered the countryside and each other. Discipline was hardly enforced, and desertions were frequent (Rankin, 12). Greene had written Hamilton, "When I came to the Army I found it in a most wretched condition. The Officers had lost all confidence in General [Gates], and the troops all their discipline . . . they were so addicted to plundering, that they were a terror to the Country" (NG Papers, 7: 89).

Yet, upon this army now rested the hopes and dreams of American freedom. Hardly a good place to start considering the consequences of failure. If the British army continued to march up through the Carolinas into Virginia everything would be lost—the declaration of independence by the American Colonies would end up on the ash heap of history.

Indeed, Greene was aware of the end game. Among his dispatches, Greene wrote of Cornwallis' intent to "prosecute his views upon Virginia" (V. Greene, 185). He had already notified Thomas Jefferson that the British intended to push through the Carolinas and occupy the lower half of Virginia. There they would wait until the terms of enlistment for the militia expired and take over the rest of that state. A force under Benedict Arnold was already in Virginia, ravaging and burning the countryside and making an attempt on Richmond. Arnold's goal was to join forces with Cornwallis when his British army arrived from the Carolinas.

General Greene, always a prolific letter writer, continuously pleaded for support for his army. Despite begging for help as he faced

Cornwallis' veteran British troops, help continued to be nonexistent. Soon after surveying the remnants of the Southern army, General Greene had no choice but to divide his army to save it, knowing that it would be easier to forage for food and supplies as two groups rather than one. Besides the majority of his troops needed to locate to a safe area to rest and recuperate. He gave Daniel Morgan instructions to take the remainder of the army westward to force Cornwallis to split his own force and try to find the Americans before they could threaten the British outpost of Ninety Six. This resulted in Daniel Morgan's decisive win over British Legion commander Banastre Tarleton at Cowpens, where Tarleton lost 90 percent of his force—the cream of the British army.

This crucial defeat of the British initiated Cornwallis' full-fledged pursuit of Morgan's army. Greene left the remaining army in South Carolina under General Huger, and raced to join Morgan as his troops headed through the Carolinas, crossing one river after another ahead of Cornwallis.

Among his pleadings Greene stressed the need for militia, but militia generally failed to turn out along the way. In one instance Greene wrote to American Colonel Locke in a letter dated January 31, 1781, apprising him that Cornwallis is on the other side of the Catawba and of the importance of militia in restraining him from further advance:

> Sir:—The enemy are laying on the opposite side of the river; and, from every appearance, seemed determined to penetrate the country. General Davidson informs me that he has called again and again for the people to turn out and defend their country. The inattention to his call and the backwardness of the people is unaccountable. Providence has blessed the American arms with signal success in the defeat of Tarleton, and the surprise of Georgetown, by Col. Lee with his legion . . . Let me conjure you, my countryman, to fly to arms, and to repair to headquarters without loss of time . . . You

have everything that is dear and valuable at stake. If
you do not face the approaching danger, your
country is inevitably lost . . . The Continental army
is marching with all possible dispatch from the
PeeDee to this place; but, without your aid, their
arrival will be of no consequence (Caruthers, 20-21).

Militia were eventually recruited by Locke, even though Cornwallis
did not meet effective resistance at Cowan's Ford. In fact, General
Davidson of the North Carolina militia was killed.

However, recruiting militia during the retreat was the least of
Nathanael Greene's worries. Along with scarce rations, blankets, and
clothing, Greene's march before Cornwallis occurred under the worst
possible conditions. The weather was horrible. His army encountered intense rain, extreme cold, rutted and muddy roads, which
mired up men, horses, and wagons, and then froze over at night into
sharp crusty edges that viciously attacked the feet of men marching
without shoes. Add to this the lack of help from either Congress or
the States with regard to reinforcements and supplies. It was a
miracle that Greene's army survived to get to the Dan River.

General Greene's hindrances were enough in themselves but
Cornwallis' army was never far behind. Caruthers states in his
*Revolutionary Incidents* that:

> The British, if they were not better fed than the
> Americans, had much better clothing and equipment
> of every kind. Their hardships and sufferings,
> however, were immense; but officers and men alike,
> bore them all with astonishing fortitude and pa-
> tience, in the hope of overtaking Gen. Greene, and
> thus putting an end to the war at once (61).

The whole country watched as this outnumbered and outgunned
American Army maneuvered across the landscape while Cornwallis'
army snarled and clawed at its every step.

George Washington Greene speaks of his grandfather's predicament and its importance in the cause of American independence in his *Life of Nathanael Greene*. He writes:

> Yet on this little army hung the fate of the South; and as men called to mind how Lincoln and Gates had failed, they trembled for Greene. How could he hope with such inadequate means to make head against the best of English soldiers, led by the best of English generals? How could he keep down the Tories, now that the royal troops were at hand to protect and incite them? How could he keep up the courage of the Whigs, with the Tories at their doors to burn and kill? Arnold was in Virginia, at the head of a strong detachment. What was there to prevent him from cooperating with Cornwallis and crushing Greene between them? Never had there been a moment of deeper anxiety. Never had the separation of north from south been so imminent. Never had men listened more eagerly for the steps of the courier, or weighed more earnestly the ground of their few hopes, and many fears! "My hopes," writes Washington to Greene, "rest on my knowledge of your talents" (166).

Col. Light-Horse Harry Lee of Lee's Legion spoke in his *Memoirs* of that "long, arduous, and eventful retreat" and how it was viewed by the nation. He noted:

> No operation during the war more attracted the public attention than did this: not only the toils and dangers encountered by a brave general and his brave army interested the sympathy of the nation, but the Safety of the South, hanging on its issue, excited universal concern. The danger of this contingency alarmed the hearts of all, especially the more reflecting, who deemed the integrity of the Union essential to American liberty and happiness, and indispensable to our future safety and strength.
>
> Destroy the army of Greene, and the Carolinas with Georgia, inevitably become members of the British

empire. Virginia, the bulwark of the South, would be converted first into a frontier, then into the theatre of war. Already drained nearly to the bottom, she would be committed into a contest for life with reduced means and broken spirits. All the country south of James river, so convenient to predatory incursions from the southern states, would soon be ground to dust and ashes. Such misery without hope could not be long endured; and reannexation to the mother country, presenting the only cure within reach, it would be solicited and obtained. The part of the state north of James river, west of the Blue Ridge, must continue united; and so far as its ability permitted, would be found a daring and destructive foe. But in this desperate condition of affairs, with the enemy's uncontrolled maritime superiority, and the facile admission into the bosom of the country, presented by its fine rivers, its resistance could not be of long duration. The stoutest heart trembled lest the Potomac should become the boundary of British dominion on the east of the Blue Ridge (293-294).

If the British could destroy Greene's army they could doubtless gain possession of the Carolinas and Virginia and at least retain that much of the American colonies. They would then be able to cut off the financial support that came from trade with European countries in tobacco, cotton, indigo, and rice. They could also prevent trade and communication with the Northern colonies. Later, an offensive might subdue even those rebels, as international support for the new nation weakened.

Despite the use of partisan groups under Thomas Sumter, Andrew Pickens, and Francis Marion (the Swamp Fox), the British almost pulled off their plan. These groups, along with Light-Horse Harry Lee's Legion, were efficient in retarding the British and harassing them during Greene's retreat, but Greene simply did not have the manpower to offer a direct challenge to Cornwallis.

By February 9, 1781, Greene's army was reunited at Guilford Courthouse and was as close to the Dan River as Cornwallis, who by then was at Salem 25 miles away. Failure stared Greene in the face like no other time. Cowpens, King's Mountain, and Greene's elusive strategy were all effective in reducing Cornwallis' forces and stretching him far beyond his supply lines, but Cornwallis still appeared strong enough to engage Greene's army and destroy it. The race continued.

In a council of war on February 9th at Guilford Courthouse, Greene and his lieutenants discussed the situation. Militia reinforcements had failed to come and with Cornwallis being so close, the council knew the American army could easily be cut off if it headed for the upper fords of the Dan. Fortunately, Greene had charged Colonel Carrington, his Quartermaster, to assemble boats at the lower fords of the river near South Boston, Virginia. After the council supported retreating to the Dan River, Greene once again divided his troops to screen his true movements in that direction. The following passage from *Rebels and Redcoats* summarizes the fears of Greene's little army and the final hours of the race.

> The next days, every officer in Greene's army knew, would see a race whose outcome might determine the fate of the South. If Greene were overtaken and defeated, Cornwallis' way would be open to a junction with the British in Virginia. Once that had been achieved, the contest in the South would be at an end.
>
> For five tense days, with his rear guard almost never out of site of the enemy's van, often drawing up to force him to deploy and then flying once more, Greene raced Cornwallis for the Dan. On the fourteenth, the mud-splattered, exhausted rebels won. When Cornwallis reached the rushing waters of the river every boat was on the farther shore.
>
> Greene's army was safe, but it was a scarecrow army, hungry, ragged and depleted of strength (507).

George Washington Greene vividly captures the moment as his grandfather's army rested across the Dan out of harm's way:

> That night the American army slept on the north
> bank of the Dan. It was long since they had slept
> so sweetly, and never had their spirits been lighter.
> And when they woke at dawn, and saw through the
> cold gray air, the paling watch-fires of the enemy
> on the opposite bank, their hearts beat high with
> exaltation; not merely that present doubt and fear
> were over; not merely that they could give rest to
> their weary limbs and satisfy to the full the
> cravings of hunger, but because their safety was the
> safety of the south, and in their own triumph they
> foresaw the triumph of their holy cause. Officer
> and soldier met with radiant smile and beaming
> eye. Around every watch-fire there were tales of
> risks run, feats performed, and privations endured.
> Loud were the praises of Williams and his gallant
> light troops, earnest the commendations of
> Carrington, who had done staff duty and field duty
> through those anxious days, and done both so well.
> But louder and more earnest still were their expres-
> sions of admiration for Greene, who had foreseen
> every danger, provided for every contingency, and
> inflicted upon the British arms the severest blow
> which they had received in the whole course of the
> southern war (173-174).

It was a magnanimous escape that rescued the revolution. Benson Lossing in his *Pictorial Field-Book of the Revolution* addressed the anxiety concerning Greene's precarious retreat before Cornwallis. He writes, "Upon this movement all eyes were turned, and when the results were known the friends of liberty everywhere chanted a loud alleluiah" (398).

By crossing the Dan River and saving the army to fight another day, Greene also discouraged further disaster for Virginia, the most crucial of the states Cornwallis wanted to conquer. W. J. Wood says:

> Greene had now been driven out of the Carolinas,
> and no longer was there an organized Patriot force
> located south of Virginia capable of fighting a
> British army. Yet, by retreating north of the Dan, the
> American general had not only saved his army but
> was still capable of preventing Cornwallis from
> marching into Virginia and linking up with forces
> there to subdue the rest of the South (238).

Greene was not totally sure that Cornwallis might not attempt further pursuit. He writes to Washington on February 15th from Irwin's ferry on the Dan River in Virginia, stating that ". . . I fear unless reinforcements come from the Northward, this will prove a devoted [meaning cursed] country" (NG Papers, 7: 294).

However it wasn't feasible for Cornwallis to continue the chase for several reasons. His army was short on supplies and provisions and was now some 230 miles from his base in South Carolina. Furthermore, Cornwallis enjoyed another conundrum:

> The depredations of his army had aroused the enemy
> of the country, and he could never hope to be
> supplied where he was. Even if he were better
> equipped and supplied, he had no boats with which
> to cross the Dan; he could not use the upper fords,
> for Greene would oppose him, and then, if necessary
> fall all the way back to eastern Virginia, join with
> Steuben and far outnumber him" (Scheer and
> Rankin, 508).

Yet, Greene himself may not have realized at that moment what had actually taken place. The magnitude of his crossing of the Dan was not evident until further events happened as a result of his action.

Though Greene might have feared not getting reinforcements, they did come and in abundance. Having faced down the barrels of over

3,000 British guns in the recent chase, Greene found himself shortly with over 4,000 men as militiamen flocked to fill his ranks from all over the region. Even though Greene's army recrossed the Dan before all reinforcements arrived, the added troops helped reverse the momentum of the Southern Campaign. Greene was now able to return to North Carolina which he had been forced to abandon. He wrote to Joseph Reed, the President of the Council of Pennsylvania:

> North Carolina has been nearly reduced as ever a
> state was in the universe . . . Our force was so small,
> and Lord Cornwallis's movements so rapid, that we
> got no reinforcements of militia and therefore were
> obliged to retire out of the state, upon which the
> spirits of the people sunk, and almost all classes of
> the inhabitants gave themselves up for lost. They
> would not believe themselves in danger until they
> found ruin at their doors" (Rankin, 280).

The British declared that Greene's army had been forced out of North Carolina but their misrepresentation of what they had accomplished would prove to be self-defeating, as their self-delusion only led to more fateful decisions. With reinforcements Greene now outnumbered Cornwallis' men, though the latter were the more battle-hardened veterans. Cornwallis was also desperate for reinforcements. He retired to North Carolina's capital of Hillsborough and proclaimed victory against Greene, hoping to enlist loyalist citizens to rally around the British ensign.

Of course, the British never conceded that they had been out maneuvered by Greene. Cornwallis, in his proclamation after retreating to Hillsborough, claimed that he had expelled Greene from North Carolina. He exulted in an empty victory with the words of his proclamation:

> Whereas it has pleased the Divine Providence to
> prosper the operations of his Majesty's arms, in
> driving the rebel army out of this province; and
> whereas it is his Majesty's most gracious wish to

rescue his faithful and loyal subjects from the cruel
tyranny under which they have groaned for many
years . . .

Other British memoirs of the war claim the same. Lt. Colonel
Tarleton stated, "The continentals being chased out of North Caro-
lina, and the militia being awed and impeded from collecting, Earl
Cornwallis thought the opportunity favorable for assembling the
king's friends. With this intention he retired from the Dan, and
proceeded by easy marches toward Hillsborough" (Tarleton, 229).
Charles Stedman, who served as Commissary under British Generals
Howe, Clinton, and Cornwallis, said in his *The History of the Origin,
Progress, and Termination of the American War*:

> Lord Cornwallis, having thus driven Greene out of
> the province of North Carolina, returned by easy
> marches from the banks of the Dan to Hillsborough,
> where he erected the king's standard, invited by
> proclamation all loyal subjects to repair to it, and
> take an active part in assisting him to restore order
> and constitutional government (332).

Frederick Mackenzie, an officer in the Royal Welsh Fusiliers wrote,
"Lord Cornwallis having pursued Mr. Greene as far as he thought
prudent, and driven him over the Roanoke into Virginia, with the loss
of all his Cannon and baggage, and many of the Prisoners taken by
Morgan the 17th of January . . ." (Mackenzie, 493).

In his proclamation at Hillsborough, Cornwallis invited those
"faithful and loyal subjects to bring their arms and provisions and
prepare to fight for the King" (Caruthers, 67). People came all right,
but not to join Cornwallis. According to British General O'Hara,
people only came to gawk at the great army encamped in the back-
woods, and having their curiosity satisfied, returned home.

Of course, the quick reentry of Greene's forces into North Carolina
probably had much to do with squelching Loyalist support.

He [Greene] recrossed the Dan on the twenty-third, and this event being made known, completely dispirited the Loyalists who were disposed to join the royal army. The recruiting service stopped, and the friends of government, awed by the fate of Pyle's corps, stood still. The situation of Cornwallis was full of peril" (Lossing, 399).

Pyle's Massacre concerned nearly 300 Loyalists beyond Hillsborough who were slaughtered by Patriot forces under Light-Horse Harry Lee and Brig. General Andrew Pickens. Needless to say, when news of that event spread around the countryside, Loyalist enlistments dried up.

In the weeks that followed, Greene's entire army continued the offensive, choosing the ground at Guilford Courthouse to engage Cornwallis. The British general readily accepted the opportunity to do battle with Greene, believing his defeat of the American army would end the resistance in the South. Though Greene's army left the field to the enemy at the end of the battle, Cornwallis had suffered enormous casualties—nearly a fourth of his army, including some of his best officers. He even had three horses shot from under him. And Bloody Tarleton lost two fingers to the surgeon's knife, not enough loss, we might add, for the butchery he did upon the citizens of the South in the name of the King.

Cornwallis again claimed victory, but in Parliament there was no such applause. A Whig leader of Parliament said, "Lord Cornwallis has conquered his troops out of shoes and provisions and himself out of troops." Henry Carrington in *Battles of the American Revolution* relates British comments on the Battle of Guilford Courthouse. The cry from Charles Fox in the House of Commons was "Another such victory would ruin the British army." William Pitt and others considered it the "precursor of ruin to British supremacy in the south." Colonel Tarleton believed that the Guilford Courthouse victory was "the pledge of ultimate defeat." And Greene himself wrote "the enemy gained his cause but is ruined by the defeat of it."

In the view of John Buchanan it was left to British General O'Hara to "paint the bleakest picture of the result of Cornwallis's failure." O'Hara wrote:

> I wish it had produced one substantial benefit to Great Britain, on the contrary, we feel at the moment the sad and fatal effects our loss on that Day, nearly one half of our best Officers and Soldiers were either killed or wounded, and what remains are so completely worn out by the excessive fatigues of the campaign, in a march of above a thousand miles, most of them barefoot, naked and for days together living upon Carion which they had often not time to dress, and three or four ounces of ground Indian corn has totally destroyed this army—entre nous, the Spirit of our little army has evaporated a good deal. No zeal or courage is equal to the constant exertions we are making. Tho you will not find it in the gazette, every part of our army was beat repeatedly, on the 15th March, and were obliged to fall back twice (381-382).

Charles Ross in his *Correspondence*, while downplaying the mauling Cornwallis received at Guilford Courthouse, tells what effect it had on the war. He wrote:

> This battle, however glorious to the British arms, was productive of little real advantage . . . The severe loss he had sustained, and the want of provisions, arising partly from the disaffection of the country, rendered it impossible for Lord Cornwallis to follow up the blow by pursuing General Greene . . . whose forces effectually prevented supplies being drawn from the open country, and, by keeping possession of the steep banks on each side of Cape Fear River, rendered it impossible to navigate boats from Wilmington. No alternative remained but to move to Wilmington (86).

Faced with this continued harassment by Greene's army, which continued to scare away Loyalist followers, Cornwallis retreated to Wilmington. He could not head south after Greene, because he would have admitted defeat in running Greene out of the Carolinas after boasting so much about it. That Greene still had an army—a larger one than Cornwallis this time—could only lead to another confrontation likely to bring further shame to Cornwallis and ultimately failure to subdue Virginia.

Cornwallis, desperate for supplies, filed off to Wilmington to rest and refit his troops and await further orders. Yet, he had his mind made up. He would go into Virginia. His mood is indicated by his correspondence with Lord Germain, General Henry Clinton, and General Phillips (whose army was in Virginia) as indicated in the letters found in *Correspondence of Charles, First Marquis Cornwallis*. He put a positive spin on his situation and refused to believe the reality of his circumstances that the game was up.

To General Phillips he writes from his camp near Wilmington April 10, 1781:

> What is our plan? I am quite tired of marching
> about the country in quest of adventures. If we
> mean an offensive war in America, we must abandon
> New York, and bring our whole force into Virginia;
> we then have a stake to fight for, and a successful
> battle may give us America. If our plan is defensive,
> mixed with desultory expeditions, let us quit the
> Carolinas (which cannot be held defensively while
> Virginia can be so easily armed against us) and stick
> to our salt pork in New York, sending now and then
> a detachment to steal tobacco & c (87).

On the same day, Cornwallis wrote to General Sir Henry Clinton, stating: "Until Virginia is in a manner subdued, our hold on the Carolinas must be difficult, if not precarious" (86).

Cornwallis wrote to Lord George Germain on April 18, 1781:

> If therefore it should appear to be the interest of
> Great Britain to maintain what she already pos-
> sesses, and to push the war in the Southern provinces
> . . . a serious attempt upon Virginia would be the
> most solid plan, because successful operations might
> not only be attended with important consequences
> there, but tend to the security of South Carolina, and
> ultimately to the submission of North Carolina. The
> great reinforcements sent by Virginia to General
> Greene, whilst Arnold was in the Chesapeak, are
> convincing proofs that small expeditions do not
> frighten that powerful province (90).

General Clinton wrote Cornwallis on April 30, 1781: ". . . If we
have force to accomplish it, the reduction of the province [Virginia]
would be of great advantage to England, on account of the value of
its trade—the blow it would be to the Rebels—and as it would
contribute to the reduction and quiet of the Carolinas (114)." It is
evident that the British intended to continue with their original plan
of subduing Virginia, despite the fact that the South was not safe and
secure from Greene's army. Clinton had not really wanted
Cornwallis to come northward until the South was firmly in British
hands, which it was not, but Cornwallis had his way.

Cornwallis had staggered into Wilmington with 1432 troops, a
fraction of the 4000 troops he started out with in South Carolina. He
was in no position to wage an aggressive campaign. Yet, Cornwallis
headed north from Wilmington to Virginia, stating to General
Clinton, "I could not remain at Wilmington, lest General Greene
should succeed against Lord Rawdon [who commanded British
forces at Camden], and, by returning to North Carolina, have it in his
power to cut off every means of saving my small corps . . ."
(Carrington, 566). Cornwallis reasoned, too, that if Rawdon took
care of Greene there would be no need for his British forces to be in
Wilmington.

The spring of 1781 saw Britain's grandiose plan of conquering the South thwarted time and again by Greene's army since it recrossed the Dan. The continual harassment of Patriot partisan groups that struck fear in the Loyalists, the mauling of the British at Guilford Courthouse, and the real possibility of Cornwallis being defeated in a battle at Wilmington all resulted in the coming surrender of the British.

General Greene with his resupplied army marched south to conquer the British outposts in South Carolina, with the help of Sumter, Pickens, Marion, and Light-Horse Harry Lee's Legion. Greene engaged British garrisons at Hobkirk's Hill on April 25, then embarked on a four-week siege of Ninety Six, and a battle at Eutaw Springs on September 8, 1781. None of these was an American victory, but they demoralized the British and forced them to retreat to the safety of Charleston. Although Greene's "ensuing operations were tactically unsuccessful . . . Greene's maneuvers resulted in strategic victory, clearing the British from the interior of South Carolina by the end of 1781" (Sarles & Shedd, 47). What is most revealing was Greene's capacity to turn seeming failures into victory. During that time he had written to French minister, the Chevalier La Luzerne, his most memorable statement of the war: "We fight, get beat, rise, and fight again" (Hibbert, 313).

Greene's army was still in the South when Cornwallis went into Virginia. There the British general surrendered at Yorktown, where his soldiers stacked their arms and their band played "When the World Turned Upside Down." This effectively ended the war though the British remained in New York and Charleston for some time.

### *Conclusion*

Greene's success in saving his army by crossing the Dan River in a march with unimaginable obstacles against a formidable enemy must be regarded as an unparalleled feat in the annals of American war history. That he saved his army against all odds, prompted George Washington to write this: "You may be assured that your retreat before Lord Cornwallis is highly applauded by all ranks and it reflects much honor upon your military abilities" (V. Greene, 175).

Crossing the Dan was a crucial moment in the Southern war that set the stage for the final outcome of the Revolution. What began as a chase by a determined enemy to capture a much-diminished American army, became a war of attrition where Cornwallis lost men continually to death, disease, and desertion and left his army short of supplies.

In every critical situation in life, a change usually revolves around a turning point, a moment when the momentum shifts the other way. Sometimes it occurs during sickness when the fever breaks. Other times, a relationship is restored as forgiveness is offered. And a situation may drastically change when truth is discovered. The pivot or turning point does not need to be a great victory; it may be something as small as a river. I once heard the story of an attempt to get a long thick rope across a deep wide gorge. No one could toss the rope across, but an ingenious way was found. An arrow tied to a piece of string was shot across, then someone pulled the string from that side. To that string was tied a thicker string, which was pulled over, and then an even thicker one until a long thick rope was pulled over easily by one not as thick. The Dan River, like that initial string in the story, was thus tied to the larger event of Yorktown, and the deliverance of the South.

Naturally, Greene's triumph does not take away either the sacrifices or the success of other leaders or minimize the final days of the war when Washington's army and the French fleet took every measure to bring about a final victory. However, the surrender at Yorktown must be seen in context, not as a lone victory. It has been said no better than by that comment attributed to an unnamed continental soldier of the Maryland Line:

> Credit is unquestionably due the army before
> Yorktown for their gallantry in compelling Lord
> Cornwallis to surrender: but while shouts of our
> fellow-citizens proclaim their triumphs throughout
> the United States, I hope that it will never be forgot-
> ten that the army of Greene took off the keen edge of
> the sword of the enemy, and made him a far easier
> conquest, than he otherwise would have been.

Greene himself wrote to Henry Knox in 1781 during the siege of Yorktown:

> We have been beating the bush and the General
> [GW] has come to catch the bird . . . The General is
> the most fortunate Man, and may success and laurels
> attend him. We have fought frequently and bled
> freely, and little glory comes to our share. Our force
> has been so small that nothing capital could be
> affected, and our operations have been conducted
> under every disadvantage that could embarrass either
> a general or an army. We have done all we could . . .

It is clear that the Race and Greene's crossing of the river became swallowed up in the greater victory of Yorktown.

It is also true that the British never saw it as more than Greene being chased out of North Carolina; it was not an important battle so much as a missed opportunity to destroy Greene's army. Besides, defensive actions like retreats just save armies; they don't deal a death-blow to the enemy. Whoever heard of a retreat determining the outcome of a war. Yet, to picture Greene's actions as merely a retreat diminishes its importance in determining the end of the war.

Another reason for the lack of importance attached to the Race to the Dan is the national admiration for George Washington. Let us not underestimate his value to the American cause. Washington was highly visible and is responsible like no one else for American independence. As Light-Horse Harry Lee said at Washington's funeral, he was: "First in war, first in peace, and first in the hearts of his countrymen." Light-Horse Harry Lee was correct. Washington should always be revered as the most magnificent hero of our history. Had it not been for George Washington we would not exist as a country. In a sense he birthed us as a nation more than any other patriot through his leadership and example. He not only held the army together, he held the country together as well.

Stories of the Revolution revolve around Washington and rightly so. Pictures from the war show Washington triumphantly crossing the Delaware and with his suffering men at Valley Forge. Greene was not in the forefront of those events, nor was he present at Yorktown. Even his outstanding service as Quartermaster General to Washington during the final days at Valley Forge was overshadowed by Washington's presence and von Steuben's role in retraining the army. Greene was always in Washington's shadow, but he never complained about Washington. To the contrary, he revered him.

Another factor minimizing Greene's accomplishment in crossing the Dan was that Greene's exploits were in the South, far from the North, the center of Revolutionary activities. After all, it was in the North where independence was said to be born, and where the Boston Massacre, the Boston Tea Party, along with the much-heralded battles of Lexington and Concord energized the Revolution. In the North too were precious and much needed Patriot victories early on at Trenton and Sarasota.

What Greene's army did was anxiety ridden for the nation during February 1781, but once he escaped the clutches of Cornwallis it wasn't news any more. Washington and Lafayette came down from the North and with the French finished off Cornwallis, while Greene continued after the small game in the South.

In time the great deed of Greene and his army faded from the public mind. There was a nation to build and a Constitution to write. Ten years after the crossing of the Dan, Otho Holland Williams, commander of Greene's Light Corps during the final days of the race to the Dan River, wrote Light-Horse Harry Lee these words: "The retreat of the southern army to the Dan River, though now forgotten, was, in my estimation, one of the most masterly and fortunate manoeuvres of our beloved Greene."

Greene's retreat, though dramatic, failed to maintain itself in the national consciousness and hardly does today. This writer knows of only one little known picture in early literature of Greene's troops crossing the Dan River—found in Benson Lossing's *Pictorial Field-*

*Book of the Revolution*. Some authors today have given little space in historical texts to Greene's race. One well known Revolutionary War television series and its companion book does not even mention it and hardly mentions the Battle of Guilford Courthouse. Yet the author devotes three pages of the book to the controversial Boston Massacre, which was not a massacre but a case of self-defense riddled throughout with misjudgments. The Boston Massacre was hardly a tactical victory of any kind that pushed the war toward conclusion though it did inflame the passions of revolution at the time.

In this writer's view there is a long-standing bias toward Northern campaigns and events of the Revolution. A fresh look needs to be taken of the war in the South to see it for the deciding factor it was in the Revolution. For instance, some events in the North have taken on a life beyond their actual significance. If a decision had to be made about which events made the most difference in the final outcome of the Revolution would it be Washington's Crossing of the Delaware or Greene's Crossing of the Dan? What was more important for the end game, surprising a Hessian army recovering from a night of celebration on Christmas Eve or delivering Cornwallis into the clutches of Yorktown? What is more important, a moral victory that has little strategic value or a retreat that leads to real victory? Despite the fact that these questions can be reasonably argued from both points of view, I believe the campaign of Greene in the Southern States must be looked at in perspective and not as a side story or as a parenthesis between other greater events.

With a stalemate in 1778 and no defeat of the British in sight, no one was transfixed on the crossing of the Delaware. The mobbing of British soldiers in Boston, which prompted them to fire into the crowd killing some of their attackers, mattered little in 1781. Even the Boston Tea Party, a powerful symbolic resistance to English taxes, though crystallizing the sentiments against the British, did not make a difference in 1778 when the war had gone on and on and many in America were tired of it, and Washington's forces remained at a standstill for a year or more.

As the Revolution continued into 1781 what ultimately mattered was that Greene crossed the Dan. Had it not been for that turning point we might all be singing "God Save the Queen" instead of "The Star-Spangled Banner."

The first to recognize the significance of what Greene had to do when he took command of the Southern army was George Washington himself. Washington understood that if something wasn't done to support and strengthen the Southern army under Greene then the war would be lost. His worst fear, previously mentioned in this essay, bears repeating: "The history of this war is a history of false hopes."

Fortunately, Washington's worst fear never happened. The bloody footprints that Greene's men left in the frozen ground on their painful march to the Dan is a reminder of how much so many owe so few.

## Bibliography

Andrist, Ralph K,. ed. *George Washington: A Biography in His Own Words*. New York: *Newsweek,* 1972.

Buchanan, John. *The Road to Guilford Courthouse*. New York: John Wiley and Sons, 1997.

Caruthers, Rev. E. W. *Revolutionary Incidents in the Old North State*. Philadelphia: Hayes and Zell, 1856.

Churchill, Winston. *The Age of Revolution*. New York: Dodd, Mead and Company, 1957.

Greene, Francis Vinton. *Great Commanders: Nathanael Greene*. New York: D. Appleton and Co, 1893.

Greene, George Washington. *The Life of Nathanael Greene*. Boston: Houghlin Mifflito and Company, 1897.

Hibbert, Christopher. *Redcoats and Rebels:* The American Revolution Through British Eyes. New York: Avon Books, 1990.

Lee, Henry. *Memoirs of the War of the Southern Department of the United States.* Vol. II. Philadelphia: Bradford and Inskeep, 1812.

Mackenzie, Frederick. *Diary of Frederick Mackenzie.* Cambridge: Harvard University Press, 1970.

O'Hara, Charles. "Letters of Charles O'Hara to the Duke of Grafton." Edited by George C. Rogers, Jr. *South Carolina Historical Magazine,* 65 (July 1964), pp. 158-180.

Owen, James. "The Site of the first eventful failure of Lord Cornwallis." *Virginia Magazine of History and Biography,* 44: (1936), 207-222.

Rankin, Hugh. *The American Revolution.* New York:  G. P. Putnam's Sons, 1964.

Ross, Charles. *Correspondence of Charles, First Marquis Cornwallis.* Vol. I. London:  John Murray, 1859.

Sarles, Frank B. and Charles E. Shedd. *Colonials and Patriots: Historic Places Commemorating our Forebears 1700-1783.* Vol. VI. Washington: National Park Service, 1964.

Scheer, George F. and Hugh Rankin. *Rebels and Redcoats: The American Revolution Through the Eyes of Those Who Fought and Lived It.* New York: DeCapo Press.  1957.

Showman, Richard K. and  Dennis Conrad, eds. *The Papers of General Nathanael Greene.* Vol. VII.  December 1780-March 1781. Chapel Hill, NC:   UNC Press, 1994.

Stedman, C. *The History of the Origin, Progress, and Termination of the American War.* Vol. II. London: 1794.

Nathanael Greene
Statue at Guilford Courthouse National Military Park

# Nathanael Greene's Southern Strategy

The British, by all appearances and statistics should have won the
American Revolution—especially during the Southern Campaign of
that war in 1780-81. At the very least they should have kept the
Southern Colonies under their rule. And who knows what might
have precipitated from that—with the British firmly in control of
New York—all the remaining Colonies quite likely would have
capitulated and the Revolution would be no more. Had that happened, the Declaration of Independence would have ended up as
wasted words on worthless paper, and its signers imprisoned or
hanged.

By the time of the Southern Campaign, George Washington's army,
though having dealt the British several major victories in previous
years, was destitute of most necessities. Beyond that, the war had
become a tiresome ordeal with no end in sight.

And the French connection, that is, their alliance with the Colonies in
1778 after the Battle of Saratoga, did little to resolve the situation at
that time. Their fleets were preoccupied with the war with England
and the subsequent power struggle in the West Indies where thriving
trade with Europe involved sugar, molasses, fruit, hardwood and
various other raw materials. Whoever controlled the West Indies
controlled the sources of these valuable products. With France and
England at war, efforts by the French to assist the Colonies appeared
halfhearted. On the other hand, these circumstances compelled the
British to send troops elsewhere to defend their interests, thus
reducing the number available for engaging the Colonists.

The war in the Northern Colonies remained stalled at the beginning
of 1778, then in the following year bad news from the South made
the hopes for American independence even more distant. On October
9, 1779, the British captured Savannah and later all of Georgia. Then
Charleston, the center of political power in the South, as well as its
major port, capitulated on May 12, 1780, when American General

Benjamin Lincoln surrendered 5,500 troops to British forces commanded by Generals Clinton and Cornwallis. On August 16, 1780,
another Southern army was crushed and humiliated at Camden,
South Carolina. Its leader, the hero of Saratoga General Horatio
Gates and many of his army bolted and ran before Cornwallis'
troops. After Camden only a skeleton American army remained—
destitute of food, clothes, munitions, wagons, and demoralized.

The eyes of the young American nation watched in painful agony as
Cornwallis continued his march through the Carolinas. Like a rabid
fox among a flock of chickens, his forces had its way. There seemed
to be no stopping him from crossing into North Carolina and then
into Virginia where he could join British General Leslie's troops
already in the Chesapeake. Together, these combined forces would
be able to invade Maryland, Delaware, and New Jersey. Washington's army, by then in a vise grip between British armies north and
south of him, would likely have been forced to surrender.

### British Advantages

The British had nearly every advantage one could ask for in conquering an enemy. Joel Woodward in *A Comparative Evaluation of
British and American Strategy in the Southern Campaign of 1780-
1781* notes that the British held Canada and remained in the Northern
Colonies. To the west the Colonists were hemmed in by the natural
barrier of mountains and wilderness. The Royal Navy ruled the sea.
With a British army marching through the South in 1780, the Americans were effectively surrounded (44).

Also, the British had anple access to more troops because they
controlled the major ports in the South. The defeat of the left wing
of Cornwallis' army at King's Mountain in October 1780 halted any
dreams of a British invasion of the western frontier and proved that
the British army was not invincible. However, in response to this
defeat, Cornwallis retreated south to Winnsborough, South Carolina,
and awaited reinforcements from General Leslie's troops from
Virginia.

According to British records for December 1780 Cornwallis controlled 10,622 British soldiers in the South, including those who occupied Charleston and others who maintained the outposts scattered across South Carolina (V. Greene, 178).

Not only did Cornwallis have many more soldiers compared to the American army hunkered down near Charlotte, but his British troops were elite units: two regiments of Guards, seven regiments of the line, the British Legion of cavalry and infantry, the brutal but efficient Hessian Jägers, the Regiment of Bose (royal artillery), several battalions of Loyalist recruits from the North, plus Tory or Loyalist militia units from Georgia, South Carolina, and North Carolina.

More importantly, the majority of these British troops were veterans who had been fighting since 1776 in battles all around New York, New Jersey, Philadelphia, and New England. In the second British invasion of the South they whetted their swords even more at Charleston and Camden, reducing the American army presence in the South to almost nothing.

Vinton Greene ranked these British troops as "the best material in the British army, well-trained, disciplined and equipped, and supplied with everything that an ample military chest could purchase" (179).

## *The American Advantage*

In the face of these overwhelming odds, the question becomes: What happened that turned the tide of the Revolution in favor of the Colonists? More specifically, what changed the momentum of the war at this point in the Revolution and brought about the British surrender at Yorktown? Ultimately, the answer comes down to one man—Major General Nathanael Greene.

John Fiske in *The American Revolution* notes General Greene's importance: "In every campaign since the beginning of the war Greene had been Washington's right arm; and for indefatigable industry, for strength and breadth of intelligence, and for unselfish devotion to the public service, he was scarcely inferior to the commander in chief" (171-172).

At the war's beginning, Greene seemed an unlikely candidate for such a role. He began as a private in a local militia force in Rhode Island, but had never fought in a battle. He had received nearly all his military training from books on the subject. Despite his youth and this lack of experience, Greene inspired confidence and was picked by the Rhode Island Legislature to command the State's troops at Boston. Still, he never led men in battle until he fought under General Washington in New York. Not only that, he had blundered terribly in allowing the surrender of over 2,800 troops and sizeable munitions at Fort Washington prior to the retreat of Washington's army across the Hudson into Pennsylvania. But that was the last time he made such a mistake. During his Revolutionary War service Greene served General Washington well as both field commander and Quartermaster General. So impressed was Washington with Greene that Washington designated him his successor as commander-in-chief should the need arise.

As a field commander Greene found in George Washington the mentor he needed to hone his skills as a strategist. Washington taught him to preserve his army to fight another day, following the maxim that an army is not defeated as long as it is still together in the field. The main lesson was not to risk more than one could afford to lose. Woodward writes, "Greene learned from Washington that preserving the army was more important than a decisive victory" (63).

Greene had been with Washington during his retreats from Long Island, White Plains and into New Jersey, and also when Washington was forced to withdraw after the battles of Brandywine and Germantown in 1777. By 1780, after four years of declared war with the world's greatest military power, and despite every loss, setback, or obstacle before him, Washington had kept his army together in the field. Without General Washington's perseverance, there would have been no need for the British to begin a Southern Campaign.

As Washington's Quartermaster General, Greene excelled at procuring supplies and material. When Greene took over these duties in March 1778, Washington's army had endured a devastating winter at Valley Forge. Greene immediately reversed the situation regarding supplies, and despite insufficient funds and an unstable currency, brought order out of chaos. He demanded and got reports of supplies and their locations; he purchased horses, tents, wagons, boats and initiated bridge building and road building operations. With the shortages alleviated and deficiencies remedied, Major General Nathanael Greene helped make Washington's army once again a mobile force.

McCullough in *1776* notes that Greene had previously offered valuable logistical advice to Washington :

> Greene had demonstrated both rare foresight and a
> marked gift for organization when he recommended
> to Washington, and Washington agreed, that a series
> of supply depots be established across New Jersey,
> along what might, of necessity, become the army's
> path of retreat, should the British make a drive
> toward Philadelphia (245).

Greene's insight proved correct in his assessment of that situation, and when the British left Philadelphia in 1778, Greene's efforts, along with those of German drillmaster Baron von Steuben, enabled Washington's army to effectively engage the British at Monmouth on June 28, 1778. By that time Greene had only been Quartermaster General for three months.

## Greene's Experience Pays Off

After being appointed Commander of the Southern Army, Greene used his experience as a Quartermaster and as a field commander to plan his strategy. Even before he left for Charlotte to take command, he prepared contingency plans, geared to keep open a route of escape and also maintain his supply lines.

Greene had General von Steuben remain in Virginia to organize command of the militia forces there due to the presence of General Leslie's British troops in the Chesapeake. He also instructed von Steuben to send southward any forces that he could collect, forward supplies, and keep communications open with the North (V. Greene, 171).

In a letter to General Stevens on December 1st and a letter to his Quartermaster Lt. Colonel Carrington, composed on December 4, 1780, after he arrived at Charlotte, Greene made sure that supplies and forage could reach his army from the north.

To Stevens he wrote that Carrington and others were to explore the Yadkin, Catawba, and Dan rivers and prepare boats for use in transportation. Using boats would save on expenses and allow for wagons and forage to be transported to the army. Greene also gave specific instructions to Carrington on building boats, which could be used for transporting needed materials, etc. General Greene knew that the procurement of supplies was dependent on being able to cross the streams that bisect the southern states.

Of course, the boats could be used to transport his army across those rivers and also provide a means of escape if necessary. The previous summer Carrington had been instructed by General Gates to examine the Roanoke River in order to determine crossing points for men and supplies, "but also with the view of insuring a safe retreat from North Carolina should such a measure, then probable, become necessary" (Bracey, 72).

These letters to General Stevens and to Colonel Carrington indicate that General Greene wanted "boats of a peculiar kind for this Service, that will carry Forty or Fifty barrels and yet draw little more Water than common Canoe half loaded" (NG Papers, 6: 512-513 ). In the letter to Carrington, Greene spells out other needs: "500 felling Axes, 5888 Pair Horse Shoes and if you have found the Dan River navigable agreeable to your Expectations, half a Ton of Boat nails for constructing bateaus . . . One Third of the nails to be deposited on the Roanoke at the most convenient Place for building the bateaus" (NG Papers, 6: 516-517). In a letter to Colonel Nicholas Long, Greene specified the need for smith tools and carpenter tools of every kind including files and cross cut saws ( NG Papers, 6: 532).

On December 8, Greene instructed Colonel Thaddeus Kosciusko, a Polish volunteer who served as Greene's chief engineer, to find a suitable place to rest and restore this newly acquired but destitute army out of harm's way.

You will go with Major Polke and examine the
Country from the Mouth of Little River twenty or
thirty Miles down Peedee and search for a good
position for the army. You will report the make of
the Country, the nature of the soil, the quality of the
water, the quantity of Produce, the number of Mills
and the water transportation that may be had up and
down the river. You will also Enquire respecting the
creeks in the Rear of the fords and the difficulty of
passing them, all of which you will report to me as
soon as possible (NG Papers, 6: 554).

Though Greene had never been to the Southern Colonies until he
took command of the Southern Army, he learned about and used the
geography of the area in exemplary fashion. Collecting information
about the rivers in the South, and the location of usable fords was
only part of it. An alternative camp for his troops was more than just
a place away from the enemy—it had strategic importance as well.
The lay of the land had an importance all its own regarding army
operations. At the chosen ground along the Peedee River, Greene
wrote to Samuel Huntington: "At present my operations must be in
the country where the rivers are fordable . . . the region of my
operations must be above the falls of the rivers until I can control the
movements of my adversary" (NG Papers, 7: 8). Vinton Greene
notes that General Greene believed it was necessary

> . . . for him to keep near the headwaters of the
> streams where they could be easily crossed, and
> where the broken nature of the country would enable
> his inferior force to make a stand. Lower down,
> where the rivers were deep and the country wide
> open, he would have no chance against Cornwallis'
> superiority of force (185).

John Buchanan notes another aspect of Greene's strategy: "His
planning for the Southern campaign was masterly. He excelled as an
organizer and an administrator" (288). Greene was capable of
making the tough decisions—hanging men for desertion or mutiny—
in order to impose discipline on a troubled army.

One facet of his organizational and administrative skills surfaced in his appointment of William R. Davie (later the father of the University of North Carolina) to be his Commissary General. Davie had raised a company of cavalry and was reluctant to leave his command. As the story goes, Davie complained that he had no experience in keeping accounts. Greene reminded him that that was not a problem, since there was no money available to keep an account of. Although Greene had little funds at the time, he knew the importance of resources and access to them, so he planned accordingly by appointing Davie as Commissary General in preparation for better days for his army.

Greene himself had balked at becoming Washington's Quartermaster General because it was not a position that received much glory, so he understood Davie's reluctance to accept the position.

But this episode reveals Greene's changed attitude about the importance of such a position and choosing the right man for the right job. He told Davie, "It is a place of great consequence to the Army; and all our future operations depend on it." Greene mentioned that Davie's "character and standing in this Country led me to believe you are the most suitable person . . . especially as you have an extensive influence among the Inhabitants, and are upon a good footing and much respected in the Army" (NG Papers, 6: 561-562).

Also, on December 4, two days after arriving at the American camp near Charlotte, Greene wrote to Francis Marion, the Swamp Fox, who commanded a partisan group in South Carolina.

> I like your Plan of frequently shifting your Ground.
> It prevents a Surprize and perhaps a total Loss of
> your Party. Untill a more permanent Army can be
> collected than is in the Field at present we must
> endeavor to keep up a Partizan War and preserve the
> Tide of Sentiment among the People as much as
> possible in our Favour (NG Papers, 6:520).

He not only showed respect for Marion's conduct of the war, he asked Marion for spies to get intelligence about British troop movements.  Greene also gave detailed instructions about the ways and means for the spies to get information and even what information to find out.

Greene's overall strategy was effective because he paid attention to administrative and organizational needs and to details relating to geography, the movement of his army, and supplies.  Greene knew that if his little army was not supplied it "must retire to the interior towards Va. or disperse and leave the enemy in peaceable possession of two southern states."  The first night, after taking command of the Southern Army, Greene studied the resources of the countryside with Colonel Thomas Polk, General Gates commissary chief, who later remarked that "the following morning [Dec 3] he better understood them than Gates had done in the whole period of his command." (Buchanan, 288, 293).

## Greene versus Cornwallis

Nathanael Greene also knew a great deal about his opponent Cornwallis since their forces had confronted one another in engagements with Washington's army in New York, New Jersey and Pennsylvania.  Of course the reverse was also true.  Cornwallis' experience with Greene prompted him to comment, "Greene is as dangerous as Washington: he is vigilant, enterprising, and full of resources.  With little hope of gaining an advantage over him, I never feel secure when encamped in his neighborhood" (V. Greene, 174).

Thus, it must have been a chagrined Cornwallis who heard the news that Greene was assuming command of the Southern army, despite the fact that Greene's new command was almost nonexistent.

As Greene neared Charlotte to assume command, he noted that the army was "Rather a shadow than a substance, having only an imaginary existence."  Greene wrote to Washington and Jefferson also, expressing that the men were "literally naked . . . starving with cold and hunger, without tents and equipage" (V. Greene, 173).

If that wasn't bad enough, in October 1780, Congress had directed that the southern army should consist of four regiments of cavalry, four regiments of artillery, forty-nine regiments of infantry, and one regiment of artificers. The regiments were to come from Delaware, Maryland, Virginia, North and South Carolina, and Georgia and total 15,000 soldiers. But this army was all on paper. It never happened (174).

Having Greene as an opponent, whether or not he had an army worth a battle, had to have increased the anxiety of Cornwallis, even more so after the Battle of King's Mountain. He had to know that the sooner he defeated Greene the better. He did not need to give Nathanael Greene time or unnecessary advantages.

Nevertheless, from the beginning Cornwallis failed to understand the war in the South and employed a strategy destined to fail. He was a successful battle captain, who understood the tactics needed to confront an opposing army on the field. But Cornwallis was no strategist. Among other things, he outran his supply lines, invaded North Carolina before South Carolina was securely in British hands, and misjudged the strength of the insurgency as well as the enthusiasm of loyalists to join forces with him.

Another mistake was that Cornwallis failed to rein in Colonel Tarleton and his murderous Legion, who terrorized the Waxhaws and other localities by slaughtering Patriot troops trying to surrender. These actions created sympathy for the Patriot cause among those who were at first only wavering toward that direction.

Then, too, General Clinton reversed his pacification program by revoking the paroles of those who surrendered at Charleston, demanding that they swear loyalty to the King instead of sitting on the sidelines. The paroles had compelled them not to engage British troops or support the Revolution. But Clinton's reversal of this policy caused a major hindrance to British takeover of the South. In one instance, Andrew Pickens who was among those paroled, rejoined the fray again and led a partisan group that caused great havoc among the British throughout the Southern Campaign.

Perhaps Cornwallis minimized all these antagonizing factors because he possessed a jittery impatience to engage the Southern army in a decisive pitched battle that would decide the war's outcome. Major Edward Hoffer in *Operational Art and Insurgency War: Nathanael Greene's Campaign in the Carolinas* says that Cornwallis thought Greene's army was the rebel "center of gravity" and destroying it would end the Revolution (20).

One cannot blame Cornwallis for his myopic approach to the Southern campaign since he had already severely defeated two American armies at Charleston and Camden. But underestimating the enemy is not a quality of a good commander.

Cornwallis misjudged Greene in his approach to the war. He found Greene elusive and unwilling to confront him with an inferior force, which may have encouraged Cornwallis even more. But Greene knew better than to engage Cornwallis head on. His two predecessors had tried that. Lincoln had surrendered at Charleston and Gates had been humiliated at Camden after trying to engage the British and gain a decisive victory. Both Lincoln and Gates pursued the wrong goal and squandered their armies in the process (Woodward, 64, 67).

Greene had a different perception of the war in the South than either Lincoln, Gates, or Cornwallis. He had something else in mind than what had gone on before; from here on out it would not be business as usual.

General Greene had written to Samuel Huntington on November 2, 1780, a month before he arrived in Charlotte, and pointed out the strategy he intended to use:

> As it must be sometime before the Southern Army
> can be collected and equipped in sufficient force to
> contend with the Enemy in that quarter upon equal
> ground, it will be my first object to endeavor to form
> a flying army to consist of infantry and horse. It
> appears to me that cavalry and Partizan Corps are
> best adapted to the make of the country and the state

of war in that quarter, both for heading and encouraging the Militia as well as protecting the persons
and property of the inhabitants (Buchanan, 292).

Woodward believes that the reason Greene desired a small mobile
force was to effectively deny the British control of the interior.

Thus, it is clear that General Greene had at least two things in mind
as part of his basic strategy: (1) mobility and (2) the use of partisan
groups already actively engaged in the theater.

### Greene Makes the First Move

As an important part of his strategy, Greene violated one of the
primary rules of warfare. He divided his vastly inferior force in the
face of a much larger and a much more superior force. To the British
that smacked of defeatism. Right before the British had captured
Fort Washington in New York, plans and communiqués by General
Washington and others fell into British hands. They revealed
Washington's plans to divide his army to counter possible British
moves. British Commander Lord Howe's secretary, Ambrose Serle,
read the letters and noted that if the Americans failed to "find spirit
to act under the encouragement of their present numbers, there is
little reason to believe that their courage will increase upon a reduction of their strength" (McCullough, 236-237). No doubt
Cornwallis, when realizing that Greene had divided his troops, likely
considered that move a source of weakness.

What Greene actually did was to force Cornwallis to act, thus taking
the initiative away from the British commander. When he arrived at
Charlotte, Greene found Gates ready to go into winter quarters,
which was a normal thing to do by both armies in the brutal winters
of the North. However, "Greene had no such plans," says Vinton
Greene. "He intended to open a vigorous campaign" (183).

Dividing the army was a gamble, but a necessary one. It also
invoked a Napoleonic principle as described by Mark Boatner—an
army divides to live and unites to fight (1018-1019). First of all,

many of Greene's soldiers were sick, lacked clothes, and in other ways were unable to fight. He had to get them to a safe haven. Washington again served as Greene's mentor. Greene had seen Washington effectively divide his own army at Long Island, and again as he prepared to leave White Plains and cross the Hudson River.

Secondly, Greene believed that dividing his own army would allow him to control events and thus change the momentum of the war. "He knew that Cornwallis designed to march into North Carolina with his main body, leaving intact the garrisons in his numerous posts," writes V. Greene, "and his only chance of delaying Cornwallis's advance while he was collecting his own army was in threatening these posts" (184). By moving a contingent of forces east to the chosen camp of repose at Cheraw, South Carolina, Greene would be within striking distance of British garrisons at Charleston and also at Camden. Although Greene had no intentions of doing so, a feint in those directions would keep Cornwallis off balance and guessing his next move. Moving troops to Cheraw also blocked any eastward advance by the British to those areas and also denied them provisions from that part of the country (Buchanan, 294).

Part of that next move was to send Brigadier General Daniel Morgan with a contingent of forces to threaten Cornwallis' western flank, especially the important outpost of Ninety Six. His forces consisted of the best units in the Southern Army: 320 Maryland infantry, 200 Virginia militia, and a regiment of light horse numbering 100 men under Colonel William Washington, General Washington's cousin. Morgan was to cross the Catawba River where he could be joined by partisan corps under General Davidson and also Thomas Sumter. His purpose was to ". . . give protection to that part of the country and spirit up the people, to annoy the enemy in that quarter, to collect the provisions and forage out of their way" (V. Greene, 184).

Greene understood that he was placing Cornwallis in a dilemma. In a letter written January 24th, General Greene explained his division of forces:

It makes the most of my inferior force for it compels
my adversary to divide his, and holds him in doubt
as to his own line of conduct. He cannot leave
Morgan behind him to come at me, or his posts at
Ninety-Six and Augusta would be exposed; and he
cannot chase Morgan far or prosecute his views on
Virginia, while I am here with the whole country
open before me (V. Greene, 185).

Thus General Greene sought to force Cornwallis to divide his troops
to counter his own decision to increase the American army's mobility
by spreading them out. Woodard argues that, "Greene understood
that the strategic value of his army was in its existence more than in
its ability to defeat its British counterpart. As long as the Southern
Army retained its mobility and strength to pose a challenge to
Cornwallis' Army, the British could not claim control of the Carolinas" (67).

### Greene and Guerilla Warfare

Greene's plan to divide his army also included making efficient use
of partisan corps. Hoffer says:

Greene viewed guerrilla operations as an essential
part of his plan. Greene realized that guerrilla
warfare could not succeed alone against the full
force of a coordinated British and Loyalist counter-
guerrilla campaign. The Southern army must always
insure that British forces could not disperse into
small mobile units capable of seeking and then
destroying guerrilla formations. Just as Greene's
army allowed guerrilla units more freedom of action,
active guerrilla operations created freedom of action
for his army (18).

To accomplish his purposes, Greene brought guerrilla leaders under
his control by not placing officers between himself and their commands and by "providing scarce weapons, clothing, food and forage

to guerrilla units." Hoffer notes further that "the most far-reaching decision, however, regarding guerrilla operations was to attach regular forces to guerrilla commands. This integration of guerrilla and regular units operating together raised guerrilla morale, fostered a spirit of unity of purpose, and did much to eliminate parochial interests" (18). Greene's approach was very effective because militiamen began coming to Cheraw to join Greene's forces there and they also added to the numbers of guerrilla groups.

Francis Marion, the Swamp Fox, operated in the eastern part of South Carolina, between the Peedee and Santee rivers; Andrew Pickens operated in the western part between the outposts of Augusta, Georgia and Ninety Six; and Thomas Sumter operated in the northwestern part, along the Broad River and its tributaries (V. Greene, 177). These units were very efficient in providing operational and tactical intelligence, protecting Greene's forces from surprise, weakening Cornwallis' army, and preventing Loyalist reinforcements from joining Cornwallis by defeating them beforehand (Hoffer, 33).

Lt. Colonel Light-Horse Harry Lee's Legion, part of Greene's regular forces, assisted Marion in interdicting British supplies along the Peedee River. Morgan's continental forces were also combined with Pickens' partisan corps, as well as various militia groups, on Cornwallis' western flank. Because Morgan and Marion were both engaged against Loyalist forces and in threatening British outposts in Cornwallis' rear, Hoffer notes that, "By coordinating his plan with guerrilla units Greene effectively surrounded Cornwallis" (20). Woodard states that the British were "overshadowed by simultaneous threats" (35).

Andrew Pickens' partisan corps also assisted Morgan at the Cowpens, and was later involved in Greene's race toward the Dan River. As Cornwallis chased Greene across North Carolina, Pickens partisans followed in the rear of Cornwallis, harassing his army. Later, after Greene recrossed the Dan River back into North Carolina, Pickens assisted Light-Horse Harry Lee's Legion in the attack on Colonel Pyle and his Loyalist militia, as they attempted to join

Cornwallis after his retreat to Hillsborough. Andrew Pickens was needed again in South Carolina and missed the Battle of Guilford Courthouse. Lee rejoined Francis Marion after the battle at Guilford and again threatened Loyalists and British outposts in South Carolina. Pickens' partisans also joined with Lee to retake Augusta and both assisted Greene at the Siege of Ninety-Six. Thomas "Gamecock" Sumter's partisans participated in the reclaiming of the South as well, by threatening British outposts.

In general, the partisan groups were to harass the enemy in any way possible. This stymied British forces in the South and inhibited Loyalist groups, who might have supplied and aided the British, from concentrating freely or rapidly enough to be of assistance to the British cause of reducing the South (Hoffer, 29). They interrupted British communications, isolated British troops at the outposts, foraged for supplies and attacked Loyalist militia. Without Loyalist forces operating effectively, a counter revolution in the back country was impossible, and the British were not able to turn conquered territory over to them for policing and defense so the British army could concentrate on the Rebel army (Hoffer, 6-7). Partisan efforts also forced upon Cornwallis the faulty idea "that the conquest of South Carolina depended on a successful invasion of North Carolina and, at last, that both Carolinas would fall if Virginia were conquered" (Pancake, 139).

The partisan groups were valuable largely because of their loose organizational structure, popular support, and familiarity with the geography. They could come together and part whenever the need. In a sense, they were farmers by day and soldiers by night (Woodard, 45-47).

Greene had recognized the importance of partisan and militia groups way before he came to South Carolina. While he did miss the Battle of Long Island due to sickness, General Greene wrote a letter to Washington on August 15, 1776, noting that new troops [regulars] sent over to Long Island were undisciplined, inexperienced, poorly armed, and poorly equipped. They had no familiarity with the local geography or lay of the land. McCullough quotes Greene, "They will not be so apt to support each other in time of action as those who have been long acquainted, and who are not only attached to each other but to the place" (152). This statement could just as easily be said of partisan groups as well as militia and provides a counter balance to the argument advanced by some that General Greene did not like or know how to use irregular or partisan forces.

## *The Chase Begins*

As a strategist General Greene was an opportunist. Woodard believes that Greene had the intuition and innate perception to take advantage of unexpected opportunities like Cowpens (77).

When Morgan advanced westward, Cornwallis did as Greene suspected and divided his forces. He sent Colonel Banastre Tarleton and his Legion of nearly a thousand men after Morgan. As Tarleton marched his men against Morgan's forces, the resulting disaster gave Morgan a major victory in which he captured, killed, or wounded 90 percent of Tarleton's men. Loaded with prisoners, Morgan advanced away from Cornwallis who was so distraught over the great loss that he decided to give chase, thus beginning the second march across the Carolinas toward Virginia. Greene in an act of personal courage left Cheraw with several men and rode through dangerous territory to join Morgan. Together they stayed ahead of Cornwallis across the Catawba and the Yadkin, after which Greene's forces were later joined together again at Guilford Courthouse.

Greene's actions, as he wore down Cornwallis' army on the march to Virginia without engaging him, is typical of the strategy of Roman General Fabius Maximus, whose delaying action against Hannibal — while denying him battle — prevented the fall of the Roman state in the second century B.C.

As both armies advanced through the Carolinas, Greene's entire operation served to draw Cornwallis farther and farther from his supply lines, while Greene's retreat toward Virginia brought him closer to supplies and reinforcements. The retreat by Greene after Cowpens shows his ability to adapt, to be flexible to fluid circumstances, and to synchronize his disparate forces accordingly. After Cowpens, Greene had Colonel Lee return to the regular army from serving with Marion and issued a call for guerrilla or partisan forces to close the country around Cornwallis. Greene also directed Brigadier General Isaac Huger, who commanded the troops at Cheraw, to bring them forward in order to reunite his army.

## *A War of Attrition*

During the chase across the Carolinas, Cornwallis stopped at Ramsour's Mill (17 miles from Cowpens) and divested his army of all unnecessary items, including clothing, wagons, and personal belongings—anything which they could destroy to make the army a light force. The determination to catch Greene and Morgan was uppermost in Cornwallis' mind. When Greene heard what Cornwallis had done, he reputedly said, "Then he is ours." Greene knew that his evasive maneuvers taxed not only the physical stamina of Cornwallis' troops but robbed Cornwallis of needed supplies. Hoffer writes:

> British soldiers were unused to the deprivations that Cornwallis' burning of their wagon trains caused. They suffered bitterly as they marched through the North Carolina mud and winter rain in pursuit of Greene's army. Colonel Marion's guerrillas cut Cornwallis' lines of supply and thus forced his army to subsist on raw Indian cornmeal (23).

Greene's strategy at this point constituted a war of attrition. It underminded Cornwallis' army slowly but surely. Combined with partisan or guerrilla tactics this reduction of the British army by attrition gave Greene a one-two punch that hamstrung the enemy. Greene's "thorough reconnaissance, his preparation of numerous supply caches, and his building of boats now paid off. The Southern Army ferried across rain-swollen rivers and creeks while Cornwallis' men had to seek and cross inundated fords against harassing fire from Greene's rear guards" (Hoffer, 23). All of these factors hindered loyalists sympathizers from joining Cornwallis and wrought unparalleled aggravation to British patience. Woodward notes, "Nathanael Greene grasped the idea that the purpose of a withdrawal is to preserve a force, but also used the operation to exhaust his British pursuers" (74).

With Greene's army reunited at Guilford Courthouse, he had a decision to make. Should he make a stand and confront Cornwallis here or continue to retreat? He called a council of war and his subordinates agreed that the army was not prepared to engage in a pitched battle with Cornwallis, who was now 25 miles away at Salem, North Carolina. Cornwallis' men were suffering from lack of food and clothing (as were Greene's men), but they were now fewer in number from deaths in skirmishes, disease, and desertions after weeks of chasing Greene across North Carolina's inhospitable countryside. The British were nonetheless superior to Greene's combined forces, and a fight at this point was too risky.

Besides, no reinforcements from surrounding militia units seemed destined to join Greene, which made the chances of a successful engagement even less. He had sent out a call to the North Carolina militia to gather their arms to join the fight, but because of the fear of British might, the militia did not come. Therefore, Greene's senior officers believed it was no time to tackle Cornwallis. The downside of this decision was that retreating further would dispirit the North Carolinians, who would see Greene's flight into Virginia as the abandonment of their state. But Greene had no choice. It was do or die.

If Greene's army headed in a northerly direction for the upper fords of the Dan River in Virginia, he would surely be caught by Cornwallis, who was equidistant from those upper fords. There appeared to be only one viable choice to make. The Dan River was 80 miles away to the northeast near present day South Boston, Virginia. If Greene's army could get to the river, the boats that Colonel Carrington had collected would allow them to cross to the other side ahead of Cornwallis.

Greene divided his forces again, this time creating a light force under Colonel Otho Holland Williams to maneuver between Greene's main forces heading toward the lower fords of the Dan and Cornwallis' forces to the west. Williams' force of 700 men was to act as a decoy and lead Cornwallis toward Dix's Ferry near Danville, while Greene crossed 30 miles away to the east at Irwin's and Boyd's ferries down stream. This tactic worked for a while, but after Cornwallis discovered the ruse, the race became a dead heat. Williams' light corps with Lee's Legion in the rear came between Cornwallis and Greene and maintained almost constant contact with the vanguard of Cornwallis' army. What this tactic did accomplish was to buy time for Greene—time to get the main body of his troops and later Williams' light corps across the river before Cornwallis' army arrived. When British troops did arrive, all the boats were on the other side of the swollen river and Cornwallis advanced no further against Greene.

It has been suggested that this tactic of leading Cornwallis on a wild goose chase across the Carolinas culminating in a crossing of the Dan River was in Greene's mind from the beginning of his Southern Campaign. It was definitely part of his contingency plans, but Greene had really hoped to confront Cornwallis before he headed for the Dan River. Vinton Greene writes:

> He [Greene] had no intention of retreating forever
> before Cornwallis. He had hoped that by the time
> the two divisions of his army were united he would
> be joined by twelve hundred or fifteen hundred
> militia, and, if so, he was determined to fight. But,
> in spite of his appeals in every direction, not a man
> had appeared (200).

Crossing the Dan River was not Greene's plan in the beginning, nor was leading Cornwallis on the long journey through the Carolinas. Vinton Greene again explains, "It has been contended that Greene's retreat was part of a deeper plan to draw Cornwallis away from his base, while Greene constantly approached his. There is no evidence of this. The retreat was forced upon Greene by Cornwallis and Greene accepted it reluctantly" (204).

John Fiske in *The American Revolution* concurs with Vinton Greene's assessment of Greene's situation at Guilford Courthouse on February 9, the day preceding the Southern Army's march to the Dan River. He writes:

> It had not been a part of Greene's plan to retreat
> farther. He had intended to offer battle at this point,
> and had sent word to Steuben to forward reinforce-
> ments from Virginia for this purpose. But Arnold's
> invasion of Virginia had so far taxed the good
> baron's resources that he had not yet been able to
> send on the reinforcements; and as Greene's force
> was still inferior to the enemy's, he decided to
> continue his retreat (257).

Greene did have hope, however, that the war might be ended soon if his own army could get more troops once he crossed the river. Accordingly, on February 10, 1781, as his army set off on the long trek to the Dan, he wrote Patrick Henry, former Virginia governor but a legislature member at that time. A portion of that letter reads as follows:

> Your influence in Virginia properly exercised at this
> important period may terminate the War greatly to
> the honor & advantage of the Southern States. If it
> is possible for you to call forth fifteen hundred
> Volunteers & march them immediately to my
> assistance, the British Army will be exposed to a
> very critical & dangerous situation.
>
> In all probability you will find me on the North side
> of Dan River. I must repeat it, the present moment is
> big with the most important consequences, &
> requires the greatest & most spirited exertions
> (paraphrased in NG Papers, 7: 270).

It appears that Greene believed such a confrontation with reinforce-ments against Cornwallis could well end the war. So the race to reach the Dan River and cross ahead of Cornwallis coupled with his own army receiving a sizeable force of volunteers was deemed by Greene as another strategic opportunity ripe with promise. This scenario played out eventually in the next phase of the campaign.

The beauty of Greene's military mind was not in a boldly conceived plan that he devised in the beginning to lead Cornwallis on this chase and then engage him far away from help or supplies. Nathanael Greene knew how to adapt, improvise, and overcome obstacles that got in his way, and see potential outcomes in events. What he did was just as effective as if he had planned it in advance and was even more impressive since he had to make a quick study of his changing circumstances.

### *Guilford Courthouse and Beyond*

Greene's actions at Guilford Courthouse illustrate the fact that his strategy changed to suit the circumstances. After failing to capture Greene before he crossed the Dan River, Cornwallis set up the king's standard at Hillsborough, North Carolina. Loyalist support did not rally to him, so he retreated toward Guilford Courthouse.

Before Greene was reinforced with militia after recrossing the Dan, he took great risk and returned to shadow Cornwallis as the British General retreated back into North Carolina. The two armies played a game of cat and mouse until they finally engaged at Guilford Court-house. Two important aspects of this phase of Greene's strategy should be noted here. These maneuvers bought time until Greene's reinforcements arrived from Virginia and also acted to deceive and confuse Cornwallis. Furthermore, Greene demonstrated his skill at being elusive:

> For the next ten days both sides sparred for position,
> Cornwallis trying to bring on an engagement and
> Greene determined to avoid one. Every night
> Greene changed his position, and every day his
> troops were in motion, until Cornwallis was equally

> bewildered as to his position and his strength, and came finally to believe that he [Greene] had between nine thousand and ten thousand men (V. Greene, 210).

After being sufficiently reinforced with troops from surrounding counties in Virginia, swelling his ranks to over 4,400 men compared to around 2,400 for Cornwallis, Greene at last fought the big battle that Cornwallis wanted, yet on ground of Greene's choosing, now that his forces were capable of fighting the British. The results were devastating. While Cornwallis held the field and tactically won the battle, perhaps the most bloody of the Revolution, Greene won a strategic victory. From 20-30% of Cornwallis' men were casualties, including some of his major officers. Greene lost men as well, but not near as many as the British. It was a hollow victory because it reduced Cornwallis' forces even further and rendered them ineffective in following Greene back into South Carolina for another battle.

Woodward concludes, "Greene realized he could accept tactical losses, as long as he avoided operational defeat. Greene understood that he was unlikely to win the war in the Carolinas, but that it was completely possible to lose the war there . . . Greene's tactical defeat [at Guilford] brought operational victory" (63,78). The Battle of Guilford Courthouse battered Cornwallis' army beyond recognition of its former invincible image and sent it in a downward spiral that ended in defeat.

Greene's strategic goal was the destruction of British power in the South. The strategic results of Guilford were several and went a long way toward that end. Hoffer sums them up: After Guilford, General Greene controlled the surrounding area of operation, increased his relative combat power in relation to Cornwallis, and achieved greater freedom of action allowing him to achieve operational ends. "These achievements describe victory, not defeat" (35). Thus when one looks carefully at the Battle of Guilford Courthouse, Greene accomplished there what he needed without destroying Cornwallis' forces or being defeated himself.

After Guilford, Greene refused to engage Cornwallis further and retreated south, leaving Cornwallis and his ailing army to march off to Wilmington and Yorktown. Greene realized that he did not have to tactically defeat Cornwallis' army in a pitched battle at Guilford or any other place to win the South. He merely had to destroy British control of what they thought they had, which at this stage were the outposts scattered across South Carolina.

From his headquarters at Colonel Ramsays on Deep River in North Carolina, General Greene sized up the situation in a letter to George Washington dated March 29, 1781:

> In this critical and distressing situation I am deter-
> mined to carry the War immediately into South
> Carolina. The Enemy will be obliged to follow us or
> give up their posts in that State. If the former takes
> place it will draw the War out of this State and give it
> an opportunity to raise its proportion of Men. If they
> leave their posts to fall they must lose more there
> than they can gain here. If we continue in this State
> the enemy will hold their possessions in both. All
> things considered I think the movement is warranted
> by the soundest reasons both political and military.
> The Manoeuvre will be critical and dangerous; and
> the troops exposed to every hardship. But as I share
> it with them I hope they will bear up under it with the
> magnanimity which has already supported them, and
> for which they deserve every thing of their Country
> (NG Papers 7: 481).

On his return south, Greene's army fought the British at Hobkirk's Hill on April 25, lay siege to Ninety Six on May 22, and fought at an extremely bloody battle at Eutaw Springs on September 8. Greene's forces lost both battles and the siege was a tactical failure as well. Yet, even though Lord Rawdon forced Greene to retreat at Ninety-Six, the British commander knew the fort could only be held tempo-rarily, and so left it and headed to safe haven at Charleston. By reducing British forces in these battles and forcing their abandonment of Ninety Six, Greene won more strategic victories. Lt. Colonel Michael Smith in *Lord Cornwallis: A Study in Strategic Leadership Failure* quotes one of Cornwallis' officers concerning Greene's back handed successes: "The more he is beaten, the further he advances in the end. He has been indefatigable in collecting troops and leading them to be defeated" (8).

Despite Greene's failure to win any battles during his advances into South Carolina, all British in the South realized their situation was untenable and eventually retreated to Charleston. Greene, with his army reduced to 1,500 men, moved toward Charleston in November to hem the British in that port city where the British began their ill-fated Southern invasion in 1780. British records show that British forces in Charleston in late 1781 numbered 9,775 including regulars, Hessians, and provincials.

Vinton Greene writes:

> That Greene should be able, with the handful of men which by courtesy was called his army, to shut this force up in Charleston and to hold them there for the remaining year of the war without any further attempt on their part to resume the offensive, is hardly less than incredible . . . The lessons of Guilford, Hobkirk's Hill, Ninety-Six, and Eutaw Springs must have made a profound impression upon the British commanders, when they allowed themselves to be reduced to impotence by a ragged and half-starved force less than one fifth their own in numbers (282).

Alexander Hamilton described Greene's ignoring of Cornwallis and the subsequent reentry of the American forces into South Carolina as akin to the great Roman General Scipio Africanus, who left Hannibal in Italy, and went to Africa to conquer the Carthaginians.

## *A Conclusion*

In this writer's view Greene's strategy is probably more responsible for Yorktown than that of General Washington. Woodward concludes, "Nathanael Greene set the conditions for Washington's ultimate victory. There is no better testament to Nathanael Greene's generalship than the epilogue to the Southern campaign that took place at Yorktown" (95).

Everything rises or falls on leadership, and Major General Nathanael Greene's leadership was no exception. He was decisive, gifted with foresight, grasped both his capabilities and his limitations, surrounded himself with stellar subordinates and motivated them to follow him. When needed, he exhibited courage, and at other times, restraint. He knew when to gamble and when to back off. He was good natured, but determined and relentless in his loyalty to the cause. His understanding of the nature of warfare in the South, and his focus on a winning strategy rather than winning battles makes General Nathanael Greene perhaps the most premier practitioner of military art in the Revolution.

Woodward writes:

> Nathanael Greene demonstrated an extraordinary capability to visualize his battlespace, articulate his vision, and synchronize diverse resources to achieve his objectives . . . In addition to his mental and conceptual skills, General Greene displayed all the modern leadership actions involving influencing, operating, and improving . . . [and therefore] . . . offers an ideal illustration of current leadership principles (95-96).

Although this writer disagrees with John Alden's initial comment in the following statement about Nathanael Greene, his words are worth reading:

> He [Greene] was not a great commander; he never won a major victory over the British. But, laboring

under many difficulties, he proved to be more than a match for Cornwallis and other British commanders in the South. He was thoughtful, methodical, steady in adversity, and cautious in prosperity. He won the respect and trust of his officers and men. It is unlikely that any other Patriot general could have accomplished more than he did in the theater of war in the Carolinas and Georgia (461) .

Alden uses other words to describe Greene—systematic but not a slave to military convention, energetic, and audacious when necessary.

Worthy of further mention is Greene's talent for handling men. Though a hands-on commander, he also gave latitude of command to partisan leaders such as Marion and Pickens. He also did this with subordinate commanders such as Daniel Morgan at Cowpens and Otho Holland Williams with his Light Corps during the final leg of the Race to the Dan. He knew how to use his subordinates in a most effective way. Otho Holland Williams, John Eager Howard, William Washington, Daniel Morgan, Light-Horse Harry Lee—they all distinguished themselves in battle, and after the war they variously became Congressmen, Senators, Governors, and Generals in their own right. They never eclipsed their commander Greene, but their light shone brighter because of him.

Edward Daves in *Maryland and North Carolina in the Campaign of 1780-1781* writes

> . . . [Greene] had a genius for the selection of his
> subordinates, and no General in the war was sur-
> rounded by a more brilliant group of officers.
> Smallwood, Williams and Howard of Maryland;
> Sumner, Eaton and Davie of North Carolina;
> Morgan, Lee, Washington, Pickens, Sumter, Huger,
> Marion, Kirkwood, Carrington—what a list in the
> rolls of honor! . . . Moreover, in this remarkable
> group of men . . . there reigned great harmony and
> we hear little of any jealousies or petty rivalries (45-
> 46).

Besides being so well served by subordinates and his use of guerilla forces, General Greene's overall strategy really boils down to two things. First, he always took the initiative in a way that gave him an advantage over the British. He did so when he divided his army before Cowpens, again when he recrossed the Dan River, shadowing Cornwallis and engaging him at Guilford, and finally when breaking off from Cornwallis and heading South to recapture British outposts in South Carolina.

General Greene's success also resides in the fact that though he had very few if any resources, he was nevertheless resourceful in many ways. In the weeks of the Southern Campaign before, during, and after the crossing of the Dan River, Greene proved himself a master of meager resources, which included both partisan and militia forces, supplies, weapons, subordinates, intelligence, mobility, and popular support.

Hoffer believes, "The genius of Greene's campaign is that he had to create what little means he had" (30). Stated another way, Woodward says, "Greene's adaptability and willingness to make the most of what was at hand were essential to his success as an operational commander" (81). He then concludes: "Nathanael Greene's insurgency war in the South can be clearly . . . understood using present military theory. It is a classic example of the application of operational art" (35).

Thus, after over 200 years, military analysts are still in awe of Greene's strategy and find it relevant for today's military campaigns, especially insurgency campaigns in the Middle East and other places where American troops find themselves engaged in unconventional war. In many ways Major General Greene paved the way for modern warfare.

## Endnotes

Alden, John Richard. *The American Revolution—1775-1783*. New York: Harper and Row, Publishers, 1962.

Army Quartermaster Foundation. *Nathanael Greene and the Supply of the Continental Army*. Accessed February 26, 2006. http://www.qmfound.com/MG_Nathanael_Greene.htm

Bracey, Susan. *Life by the Roaring Roanoke: A History of Mecklenburg County, Virginia*. Mecklenburg County Bicentennial Commission, 1977.

Buchanan, John. *The Road to Guilford Courthouse: The American Revolution in the Carolinas*. New York: John Wiley and Sons, Inc., 1997.

Davies, Edward Graham. *Maryland and North Carolina in the Campaign of 1780-1781*. Baltimore, MD: J. Murphy, 1893.

Fiske, John. *The American Revolution*. New York: Houghton Mifflin, 1891.

Greene, Francis Vinton. *Great Commanders: General Greene*. New York: D. Appleton and Company, 1897, reprinted by Heritage Books, Bowie, MD, 2002.

Hoffer, Edward E. "Operational Art and Insurgency War: Nathanael Greene's Campaign in the Carolinas." Master's thesis. Fort Leavenworth: Command and General Staff College, 1988.

McCullough, David. *1776*. New York: Simon and Schuster, 2005.

Pancake, John S. *The Destructive War: The British Campaign in the Carolinas, 1780- 1782*. Tuscaloosa, AL: The University of Alabama Press, 1985.

Smith, Michael. "Lord Charles Cornwallis: A Study in Strategic Leadership Failure." Master's thesis. Carlisle Barracks, PA: U.S. Army War College, 2001.

Showman, Richard K. and Dennis Conrad., eds. *The Papers of General Nathanael Greene*, Vol. VI June-December 1780. Chapel Hill, NC: UNC Press, 1991.

_____. *The Papers of General Nathanael Greene*, Vol. VII December 1780-March 1781. Chapel Hill, North Carolina: UNC Press, 1994.

Woodward, Joel A. "A Comparative Evaluation of British and American Strategy in the Southern Campaign of 1780-1781." Master's thesis. Fort Leavenworth, KS: United States Army Command and General Staff College, 2002.

---

We have been beating the bush and the General [GW] has come to catch the bird . . . The General is the most fortunate Man, and may success and laurels attend him. We have fought frequently and bled freely, and little glory comes to our share. Our force has been so small that nothing capital could be affected, and our operations have been conducted under every disadvantage that could embarrass either a General or an army. We have done all we could.

— Major General Nathanael Greene
to Henry Knox on September 29, 1781,
during the Siege of Yorktown

# A Letter from Earl Cornwallis
# to Lord George Germain, Colonial Secretary
# March 17, 1781, at Guilford

My Lord,

Having occasion to dispatch my aid-de-camp, Captain Brodrick, with the particulars of the action of the 15th, in compliance with general directions from Sir Henry Clinton, I shall embrace the opportunity to give your lordship an account of the operations of the troops under my command previous to that event, and of those subsequent, until the departure of Captain Brodrick.

My plan for the winter's campaign was to penetrate into North Carolina, leaving South Carolina in security against any probable attack in my absence. Lord Rawdon, with a considerable body of troops, had charge of the defensive, and I proceeded about the middle of January upon the offensive operations. I decided to march by the upper in preference to the lower roads leading into North Carolina, because fords being frequent above the forks of the rivers, my passage there could not easily be obstructed; and General Greene having taken post on the Pedee, and there being few fords in any of the great rivers of this country below their forks, especially in winter, I apprehended being much delayed, if not entirely prevented from penetrating by the latter route.

I was the more induced to prefer this route, as I hoped in my way to be able to destroy or drive out of South Carolina the corps of the enemy commanded by General Morgan, which threatened our valuable district of Ninety Six: And I likewise hoped, by rapid marches to get between General Greene and Virginia, and by that means force him to fight without receiving any reinforcement from that province; or, failing of that, to oblige him to quit North Carolina with precipitation, and thereby encourage our friends to make good their promises of a general rising, to assist me in re-establishing His Majesty's government.

The unfortunate affair of the 17th of January was a very unexpected and severe blow; for, besides reputation, our loss did not fall short of six hundred men: However, being thoroughly sensible that defensive measures would be certain ruin to the affairs of Britain in the southern colonies, this event did not deter me from prosecuting the original plan. That General Greene might be uncertain of my intended route as long as possible, I had left General Leslie at Camden, until I was ready to move from Wynnesborough, and he was not within a day's march of me: I employed the 18th (a.) in forming a junction with him, and in collecting the remains of Lieutenant-colonel Tarleton's corps; after which, great exertions were made by part of the army, without baggage, to retake our prisoners, and to intercept General Morgan's corps on its retreat to the Catawba; but the celerity of their movements, and the swelling of numberless creeks in our way, rendered all our efforts fruitless.

I therefore assembled the army on the 25th (b.) at Ramfoure's mill, on the fourth fork of the Catawba; and as the loss of my light troops could only be remedied by the activity of the whole corps, I employed a halt of two days in collecting flour, and in destroying superfluous baggage, and all my waggons, except those loaded with hospital stores, salt, and ammunition, and four reserved empty in readiness for sick or wounded. In this measure, though at the expence of a great deal of officers' baggage, and of all prospect in future of rum, and even a regular supply of provisions to the soldiers, I must, in justice to the army, say, that there was the most general and cheerful acquiescence.

In the mean time the rains had rendered the north Catawba impassable; and General Morgan's corps, the militia of the rebellious counties of Rowan and Mecklenburg under General Davidson, or the gang of plunderers usually under the command of General Sumpter, not then recovered from his wounds, had occupied all the fords in a space of more than forty miles upward from the fork. During its height, I approached the river by short marches, so as to give the enemy equal apprehensions for several fords; and after having procured the best information in my power, I resolved to attempt the passage at a private ford, then slightly guarded, near M'Cowan's ford, on the morning of the 1st of February.

Lieutenant-colonel Webster was detached with part of the army and all the baggage to Beattie's ford, six miles above M'Cowan's, where General Davidson was supposed to be posted with five hundred militia, and was directed to make every possible demonstration, by cannonading and otherwise, of an intention to force a passage there; and I marched at one in the morning, (c.) with the brigade of guards, regiment of Bose, 23d, two hundred cavalry, and two three-pounders, to the ford fixed upon for the real attempt.

The morning being very dark and rainy, and part of our way through a wood where there was no road, one of the three pounders in front of the 23d regiment and the cavalry overset in a swamp, and occasioned those corps to lose the line of march; and some of the artillery men belonging to the other gun, (one of whom had the march) having stopped to assist, were likewise left behind. The head of the column in the meanwhile arrived at the bank of the river, and the day began to break. I could make no use of the gun that was up, and it was evident, from the number of fires on the other side, that the opposition would be greater than I had expected: However, as I knew that the rain then falling would soon render the river again impassable, and I had received information the evening before, that General Greene had arrived in General Morgan's camp, and that his army was marching after him with the greatest expedition, I determined to desist from the attempt; and therefore, full of confidence in the zeal and gallantry of Brigadier-general O'Hara, and of the brigade of guards under his command, I ordered them to march on, but, to prevent, confusion, not to fire until they gained the opposite bank. Their behaviour justified my high opinion of them; for a constant fire from the enemy, in a ford upwards of five hundred yards wide, in many places up to their middle, with a rocky bottom and strong current, made no impression on their cool and determined valour, nor (d.) checked their passage. The light infantry landing first, immediately formed, and in a few minutes killed or dispersed everything that appeared before them; the rest of the troops forming, and advancing in succession. We now learned that we had been opposed by about three hundred militia that had taken post there only the evening before, under the command of General Davidson. Their general and two or three other officers were among the killed; the

113

number of wounded was uncertain; a few were taken prisoners. On our side, Lieutenant-colonel Hall and three men were killed, and thirty-six wounded, all of the light infantry and grenadiers of the guards. By this time the rear of the column had joined; and the whole having passed with the greatest dispatch, I detached Lieutenant-colonel (e.) Tarleton, with the cavalry and twenty-third regiment, to pursue the routed militia. A few were soon killed or taken; and Lieutenant-colonel Tarleton having learned that three or four hundred of the neighbouring militia were to assemble that day at Tarrant's house, about ten miles from the ford, leaving his infantry, he went on with his cavalry, and finding the militia as expected, he with excellent conduct and great spirit attacked them instantly, and totally routed them, with little loss on his own side, and on theirs, between forty and fifty killed, wounded, or prisoners. This stroke, with our passage of the ford, so effectually dispirited the militia, that we met with no farther (f.) opposition on our march to the Yadkin, through one of the most rebellious tracts in America.

During this time the rebels having quitted Beatty's ford, Lieutenant-colonel Webster was passing his detachment and the baggage of the army; this had become tedious and difficult, by the continuance of the rain, and the swelling of the river; but all joined us soon after dark, about six miles from Beatty's ford. The other fords were likewise abandoned by the enemy: The greatest part of the militia dispersed; and General Morgan with his corps marched all that afternoon and the following night towards Salisbury. We pursued next morning, in hopes to intercept him between the rivers; and after struggling with many difficulties, arising from swelled creeks and bad roads, the guards came up with his rear, in the evening of the 3d, routed it, and took a few waggons at the Trading ford of the Yadkin. He had passed the body of the infantry in flats, and his cavalry and waggons by the ford, during that day and the preceding night; but at the time of our arrival, the boats (g.) were secured on the other side, and the ford had become impassable. The river continuing to rise, and the weather appearing unsettled, I determined to march to the upper fords, after procuring a small supply of provisions at Salisbury: This, and the height of the creeks in our way, detained me two days; and in that time, Morgan having quitted the banks of the river, I had information from our friends, who crossed in canoes, that General Greene's army was marching with the utmost dispatch to form a junction with him at Guilford. Not having had time to collect the North-Carolina militia, and having received no reinforcement from Virginia, I concluded he would do every thing in his power to avoid an action on the south side of the Dan; and it being my interest to force him to fight, I made great expedition, and got between him and the upper fords; and being assured that the lower fords are seldom practicable in winter, and that he could not collect many flats at any of the ferries, I was in great hopes that he would not escape me without receiving a blow. Nothing could exceed the patience and alacrity of the officers and soldiers under every species of hardship and fatigue, in endeavouring to overtake them: But our intelligence upon this occasion was exceedingly defective; which, with heavy rains, bad roads, and the passage of many deep creeks, and bridges destroyed by the enemy's light troops, rendered all our exertions vain; for, upon our arrival at Boyd's ferry on the 12th, we learned, that his rear guard had got over the night before, his baggage and main body having passed the preceding day at that and the neighbouring ford, where more flats had been collected than had been represented to me as possible.

My force being ill suited to enter by that quarter so powerful a province as Virginia, and North Carolina being in the utmost confusion, after giving the troops a halt of a day, I proceeded by easy matches to Hillsborough, where I erected the King's standard, and invited, by proclamation, all loyal subjects to repair to it, and to stand forth and take an active part in assisting me to restore order and constitutional government. As a considerable body of friends were said to reside between the Haw and Deep rivers, I detached Lieutenant-colonel Tarleton on the 23d, (k.) with the cavalry and a small body of infantry, to prevent their being interrupted in assembling. Unluckily a detachment of the rebel light troops had crossed the same day, and, by accident, fell in with about two hundred of our friends, under Colonel Pyle, on their way to Hillsborough, who, mistaking the rebels for Lieutenant-colonel Tarleton's corps, allowed themselves to be surrounded, and a number of them were most inhumanly butchered, when begging for quarter, without making the least resistance. The same day I had certain intelligence that General Greene, having been reinforced, had recrossed the Dan, which rendered it imprudent to separate my corps, occasioned the recall of Lieutenant-colonel Tarleton's detachment; and forage and provisions being scarce in the neighbourhood of Hillsborough, as well as the position too distant (upon the approach of the rebel army) for the protection of the body of our friends, I judged it expedient (1.) to cross the Haw, and encamped near Allamance creek, detaching Lieutenant-colonel Tarleton, with the cavalry, light company of the guards, and one hundred and fifty men of Lieutenant-colonel Webster's brigade, a few miles from me on the road to Deep river, more effectually to cover the country.

General Greene's light troops soon made their appearance; and on the 2d, a patrole having reported that they had seen both cavalry and infantry near his post, I directed Lieutenant-colonel Tarleton to move forward with proper precautions, and endeavour to discover the designs of the enemy. He had not advanced far when he fell in with a considerable corps, which he immediately attacked and routed; but being ignorant of their force, and whether they were supported, with great prudence desisted from the pursuit. He soon learned from prisoners that those he had beat were Lee's legion, three or four hundred back mountainmen under Colonel Preston, with a number of militia; and that General Greene, with a part of his army, was not far distant. Our situation for the former few days had been amongst timid friends, and adjoining to inveterate rebels; between them I had been totally destitute of information, which lost me a very favourable opportunity of attacking the rebel army. General Greene fell back to Thompson's house, near Boyd's ford, on the Reedy fork; but his light troops and militia still remained near us; and as I was informed that they were posted carefully at separate plantations for the convenience of substituting, I marched on the 6th to drive them in, and to attack (m.) General Greene, if an opportunity offered. I succeeded completely in the first; and at Wetzell's mill, on the Reedy fork, where they made a stand, the back mountainmen and some militia suffered considerably, with little loss on our side; but a timely and precipitate retreat over the Haw prevented the latter. I knew that the Virginia reinforcement were upon their march; and it was apparent that the enemy would, if possible, avoid risquing an action before their arrival.

The neighbourhood of the fords of the Dan in their rear, and the extreme difficult of subsisting my troops in that exhausted country putting it out of my power to force them, my resolution was to give our friends time to join us, by covering their country as effectually as possible, consistent with the subsistence of the troops, still approaching the communication with our shipping in Cape-Fear river, which I saw it would soon become indispensably necessary to open, on account of the sufferings of the army from the want of supplies of every kind; and at the same time I was determined to fight the rebel army, if it approached me, being convinced that it would be impossible to succeed in that great object of our arduous campaign, the calling forth the numerous loyalists of North Carolina, whilst a doubt remained on their minds of the superiority of our arms. With these views, I had moved to the Quakers' meeting, in the forks of the Deep river, on the 13th, and on the 14th I received the information which occasioned the movement that brought on the action at Guildford, of which I shall give your lordship an account in a separate letter.

I have the honour to be, &c.
CORNWALLIS

From Lt. Colonel Banastre Tarleton's *A History of the Campaigns of 1780 and 1781, in the Southern Provinces of North America.* London, 1787, pages 260-267. Available online through www.banastretarleton.org.

Greene's Crossing of the Dan
(Engraving from Lossing's *Pictorial Field-Book of the Revolution*)

# Excerpts From Seymour's Journal of the Southern Expedition

The following excerpt from Sergeant-Major Seymour's diary covers the time from Cowpens until Cornwallis retreated from the Dan River to Hillsborough, North Carolina.

In the action [Cowpens] were killed of the enemy one hundred and ninety men, wounded one hundred and eighty, and taken prisoners one Major, thirteen Captains, fourteen Lieutenants, and nine Ensigns, and five hundred and fifty private men, with two field pieces and four standards of colours. Their heavy baggage would have shared the same fate, if Tarleton, who retreated with his cavalry, had not set fire to it, burning up twenty-six wagons. This victory on our side cannot be attributed to nothing else but Divine Providence, they having thirteen hundred in the field of their best troops, and we not eight hundred of standing troops and militia.

The troops engaged against us were the 7th or Royal English Fuzileers, the First Battalion of the 71st, and the British Legion, horse and foot.

The courage and conduct of the brave General Morgan in this action is highly commendable, as likewise Colonel Howard, who all the time of the action rode from right to left of the line encouraging the men; and indeed all the officers and men behaved with uncommon and undaunted bravery, but more especially the brave Captain Kirkwood and his company, who that day did wonders, rushing on the enemy without either dread or fear, and being instrumental in taking a great number of prisoners.

Our loss in the action were one Lieutenant wounded, and one Sergeant and thirty-five killed and wounded, of which fourteen were of Captain Kirkwood's Company of the Delaware Regiment.

On the 18th we marched off with the prisoners, directing our course for Salisbury; having crossed the Catabo River on the 23rd at Shreve's Ford, and there waited for the prisoners who went another road. On our way hither we had very difficult marching, being very mountainous, the inhabitants, who were chiefly Virginians, living very poor, except one settlement on the other side the Catabo, being excellent good land and inhabited by the Dutch. We remained on this ground till the first February, waiting the motion of the enemy, who this day crossed the river lower down than where we lay, and coming unawares on the militia commanded by Genl. Davidson, on which ensued a smart skirmish in which General Davidson was killed, and a great many more killed and wounded, upon which the militia retreated off in great disorder.

We marched off this place for Salisbury on the evening of the first February, and continued our march all night in a very unpleasant condition, it having rained incessantly all night, which rendered the roads almost inaccessible.

Next day, being the 2d, we arrived at Salisbury and crossed the River Yatkin, which the enemy approached on the 3d, consisting of about six thousand men, commanded by Lord Cornwallis and General Lesley, in order to facilitate their way to Virginia and relieve General Arnold, who was blocked up in Portsmouth with about fifteen hundred men, so that he could not possibly get off without being taken prisoner with all his army.

On the 4th we received intelligence that the enemy had crossed the river at a shallow ford above where we lay, upon which we marched all that night, taking the road towards Guilford Court House, which we reached on the 6th.

Here General Greene's Army assembled on the 5th from Chiraw Hills, and in a most dismal condition for the want of clothing, especially shoes, being obliged to march, the chief part of them, barefoot from Chiraw Hills. Here however the men were supplied with some shoes, but not half enough.

On the eighth instant we marched from here, General Greene's Army taking one road and the light troops another, being joined the next day by Colonel Lee's horse and infantry. This day we received intelligence that the British Army was advancing very close in our rear, upon which Colonel Lee detached a party of horse to intercept them, who meeting with their vanguard, consisting of an officer and twenty men, which they killed, wounded and made prisoners, all but one man.

We marched from here on the ninth inst., taking the road towards Dan River, which we reached on the fourteenth, after a march of two hundred and fifty miles from the time we left our encampment at Pacolet River. By this time it must be expected that the army, especially the light troops, were very much fatigued both with traveling and want of sleep, for you must understand that we marched for the most part both day and night, the main army of the British being close in our rear, so that we had not scarce time to cook our victuals, their whole attention being on our light troops.

On the fourteenth all our troops assembled at Dan River, Virginia, which we crossed at two different ferries, viz., that of Boyd's and Irvin's.

On the seventeenth our army marched and crossed the Banister River. Here we halted till the 20th, and marched for Hillsborough, which the enemy had taken possession of, there erecting the Royal Standard, where a vast number of the inhabitants joined them, taking the oath of allegiance, and many more they compelled to do the same, forcing them away from their wives and children.

Source: *A Journal of the Southern Expedition 1780-1783* by William Seymour, Sergeant-Major of the Delaware Regiment. This journal in its entirety is available online at http://battleofcamden.org/seymour.htm.

---

. . . without baggage, necessaries, or provisions of any sort for officer or soldier, in the most barren, inhospitable, unhealthy part of North America, opposed to the most savage, inveterate, perfidious, cruel enemy, with zeal and with bayonets only, it was resolved to follow Greene's army to the end of the world.

—Brigadier General Charles O'Hara to the Duke of Grafton, April 20, 1781.

# Part II
## The Celebration

. . . In roughly six weeks an under-
manned, ill-equipped, demoralized
army reversed America's fortunes and
recaptured a large part of the South.
Makes crossing the Delaware on
Christmas eve seem like child's play by
comparison . . .

—Dr. Dennis Conrad
Editor of the *Nathanael
Greene Papers*

# Dedication of the Crossing of the Dan River Memorial in South Boston, Virginia
## 13 February 1999
## Dr. Dennis Conrad

Shortly after Nathanael Greene was named to command American forces in the South in late 1780, his friend, the poet JOM Trumbull, wrote him saying—certainly in a facetious vein-that, with all his "Talents for Warr," Greene was still "deficient in the great Art of making a timely retreat." In July 1781, Greene wrote to him and Trumbull's mutual friend, Jeremiah Wadsworth, saying: "I hope I have convinced the World to the contrary, for there are few Generals that has run oftner, or more lustily than I have done." But, Greene added, "I have taken care not to run too farr; and commonly have run as fast forward as backward, to convince our Enemy that we were like a Crab, that could run either way" (NG to Wadsworth, 18 July 1781, CtHi).

If it wasn't too esoteric a symbol, it might be well to add a small crab statue to the beautiful memorial that you have erected because like a crab, the Southern army scuttled across the Dan to save itself and just a week later, scuttled back across the Dan River to begin the advance that would, some ten months later, reclaim the entire lower South for America.

One of the most enduring images of the American Revolution is Emanuel Leutze's painting of Washington Crossing the Delaware. Though mocked for its numerous historical inaccuracies, it has become such a cultural icon that everyone assumes that the crossing of the Delaware River and the subsequent Battle of Trenton—which Nathanael Greene was one of the heroes of, by the way—was a turning point of the Revolution. Since history teachers no longer teach wars, the standard one day lesson on the American Revolution discusses the opening of the war at Lexington and Concord, the "nadir" at Valley Forge, the turn around in American fortunes beginning with the crossing of the Delaware and the Battle of Trenton and culminating the next year with Burgoyne's surrender at Saratoga, and the final victory at Yorktown.

The events that you have commemorated here are rarely even mentioned. This oversight, however, is ridiculous. The crossing of the Dan River far overshadows the crossing of the Delaware in significance, and the subsequent battle of Guilford Court House was really the event that directly led to Lord Cornwallis's surrender at Yorktown. Or as Greene put it in a letter to his friend Henry Knox, as the siege was moving into its final stage: "to take a General who has been the terrour of the South and oblige his Army to pile their Arms, will be a rich feast even for the eyes of a prince. We have been beating the bush and the General [George Washington] has come to catch the bird. Never was there a more inviting object to glory. The General is a most fortunate Man, and may success and laurels attend him. We have fought frequently and bled freely, and little glory comes to our share. Our force has been so small that nothing capital could be effected, and our operations have been conducted under every disadvantage that could embarrass either a General or an Army. We have done all we could, and if the public and our friends are not satisfied we cannot help it. We have been in such a situation that I fancy few would have thought of operating offensively, but I thought it the safest way, and even our own officers who were at first alarmed at our plan of operations are pleased at the dangers through which they have been led." (NNPM)

While Greene's words reflect some momentary bitterness, his complaint about the accomplishments of the Southern army being under appreciated was true then and is still true today. People do not realize the desperate shape the war in the South was in when Greene arrived to take command in December 1780. In spring of that year, the British had captured Charleston and the entire Southern Conti-nental army. At the surrender, depending on whose numbers you accept, between 3,300 and 5,500 American fighting men laid down their arms and became prisoners of war. Hundreds of others in the backcountrys of South Carolina and Georgia also came in and "made peace" with the British. It was the single greatest American disaster of the war and constituted the largest single surrender of American soldiers until the Civil War. To recoup, North Carolina mounted a heroic effort of raising men and material, and Congress sent Horatio Gates, considered at the time to be America's greatest general, to reverse the disaster. On 16 August, Gates' army encountered Cornwallis' near Camden, S.C., and was completely defeated. Of the 4,000 who comprised Gates' army, only 700 reached the rallying point at Hillsborough and lost nearly all the materiel that had almost bankrupted North Carolina to collect.

Therefore, when Greene took command, the Americans had lost two whole armies, the British were in control of two states, North Carolina had been stripped bare of resources and was, for all intents and purposes, out of the war, and the British had begun an invasion into Virginia, the goal of which was to interdict American supply lines—a strategy that they successfully executed through much of 1781. In the words of English historian, George Trevelyn, the American situation in the South was "a morass of troubles that seemed to have neither shore nor bottom," or in contemporary parlance "we were in a world of hurt." Let me also discuss one last consideration, which seems lost on those who now look at the war. While war-weariness was beginning to affect Britain and there had been feelers extended concerning negotiations, the idea was that any peace would be on the basis of uti posseditis, which essentially means you keep what you have when the shooting stopped. Can you imagine how our history would have been changed had the British claimed the entire lower South as their domain in a settlement of the war.

I have gone on long here to show you how desperate the American situation was when Greene took command in the South. But he and his army, in a miraculously short period of time, completely reversed the situation. First the over-the-mountain militiamen defeated Patrick Ferguson at King's Mountain and stalled one British advance, then Greene's subordinate, Daniel Morgan, defeated Banastre Tarleton at the Battle of Cowpens on 17 January. These were important victories, especially Morgan's, but Cornwallis and his army, as NG wrote Congress on 31 January, after the Battle of Cowpens, "are in force and appear determined to penetrate the Country, nor can I see the least prospect of opposing them with the little force we have, naked and distressed as we are for want of provision & forage. Our numbers are greatly inferior to the enemy's when collected and joined by all the Militia in the field, or that we have even a prospect of getting. The difference in the equipment and discipline of the troops give the enemy such a decided superiority that we cannot hope for anything but a defeat. And the enemy being with out baggage we cannot avoid an action if we would, especially as we have no place where we can take post for want of provision and forage. I have made use of every argument in my power to induce the Southern States to take decided measures for affording speedy reinforcements to this Army; but little or nothing is done, and succour appears almost as remote as when I took the ~ command. Whatever Misfortunes may happen to this Army and these States, I hope it will be found I have left nothing unattempted for the security of one and the protection of the other; and Providence has blessed the American Arms in this department with more success than we had reason to expect in our miserable situation."

Greene rode across the breadth of South Carolina with an escort of only three men and took command of Morgan's force, already retreating. He also ordered the rest of the army, then camped on the Pee Dee River in the Cheraws region of South Carolina, to begin a movement northward with the planned link-up being first at Salisbury, and then at Guilford. It was at Guilford on 9 February, that Greene made the decision to take his army across the Dan River into Virginia. Sending his light troops under Otho Williams—who replaced Morgan, who broken down with sickness, at headed home to Virginia—to feint toward the northwest, Greene and his troops headed for Irwin's and Boyd's ferries on the Dan. This retreat, remember, is not like one you see in the movies where a squad grabs its weapons and pulls back. The Southern army had to carry with it a mountain of supplies because Greene had no safe storage depot to leave them at and an eighteenth century army was like a small town. Also there were wives and, sometimes, even children with the army. On one occasion, Greene ordered that the women with the army be provided with transportation during the army's move to a new campsite. (I should also mention that on at least three other occasions Greene specifically ordered that women not be allowed to take

128

up space in the army's wagons.) The men, moreover, were in rags and shoeless and supposedly the retreat could be tracked by the blood dotting the frozen mud over which the army had passed. Cornwallis, by contrast, had a numerically superior, better-equipped army and had made the then-radical decision to destroy his army's supply train so he could move that much faster. In a sense, Cornwallis turned his army from a long-distance runner into a sprinter. He would sacrifice endurance, or staying power, for speed and a "quick-strike capability." Even though Cornwallis was fooled into believing that the American army was heading northwest, he soon understood that such was not the case and the race began in earnest. For the next three days, the van of Cornwallis's army and the rear-most unit of NG's army, Henry Lee's Legion, remained in almost constant sight of one another. To give you a sense of the tension felt by the American commanders during this dramatic retreat, I will read a letter from Otho Williams to Greene, dated 13 February:

From Colonel Otho H. Williams

Dear Genl          Coll Moores [N.C.] 7 oClock pm.

Tuesday 13th Feby 1781 wrote you to Day from
Harts old Stores where the En[emy] halted this
evening. The Express was detain'd 'till I got Coll
Lees last report and was not sent off 'till I arriv'd
here. I recd yours datd at Dobbins a little before. I
had concluded that my Letter from Chambers Mill
wod induce you to order the Army to move very
early this morning and was [exceeding]lly concern'd
to hear by the Express, before I had time to read
your Letter, that you were yet 25 miles from the
ferry. My Dr General at Sun Down the Enemy were
only 22 miles from you and may be in motion now
or will most probably by <3> oClock in the morning. Their Intelligence is good. They manouvred us
from our Strong position at <Cha>mbers Mill and
then mov'd with great rapidity. They were at Harts

Stores in a very short time after I clos'd my Letter there.

I believe it practicable for the Light Troops to remain in the State, but if we file off now it must be by the right. The Van of one of the <Enemy's Columns is not more> than ten miles in my rear and I have reason to believe there may be another on the way to Dixe's. This situation will prevent my taking the upper Country and I think the Enemy too near you for me to quit the interval. Rely on it, my Dr Sir it is possible <for you> to be overtaken before you can cross the Dan even if you had 20 Boats, and your present situation obliges me to lay within reach or Surprizeing distance of the Enemy. I shall use every precaution but cannot help being uneasy. I conclude you march'd as far to day as you cod and if your Army can make but Eleven miles in a Day you will not be able to pass the ferry in less than two Days more. In less time than that we will be dri<ven in> to your Camp or I must risque the Troops I've the Honor to command and in doing that I risque every thing[.] You know the consequence it will be to the Army and every body knows retreating Troops must suffer in the consequences however hardy they may be in their Opposition.

The G<entlemen of> Cav<alry assu>re me their Horses want refreshment exceedingly and our Infantry are so excessively fatigu'd that I'm confident I loose men every Day. We have been all this Day almost in presence of the Enemy but have sustain'd no loss but of Sick and Strollers. As to Militia, only one Coll and one Captain have joined us and their Spirits wod be better if we were farther from the Enemy. The Enemy are undoubtedly reinforcing their Cavalry by taking all the best Horses in the Country and perhaps are not so con-

temptible as we suppose them. I must beg your
permission to send my Invalids to pass at Boyds
[Ferry] and I will dispose of the rest <of the> Troops
according to your future instruct<ions.> I'm confident we may remain in the State but whither it will
not be at the risque of our Light Corps and whither
we shall not be wasted by continual fatigue you can
determine (OLC; parts in brackets, CSmH).

Soon after writing this letter, Otho Williams spied campfires ahead of
his force and thought that he had overtaken Greene's main force and
contemplated a suicidal attack on Cornwallis' army in a desperate
attempt to save the main body. Before he gave the orders, he discovered that the fires were not for Greene's army but had been left
burning for the use of Williams' men. Even more telling, however, is
the fact that Williams and his men were unable to make use of them.
So close were the pursuing British that the light troops were not able
to halt and cook a meal but had to keep marching, eating cold rations
as they went. Men slept in the saddle and probably while they
walked, which, according to Steven Ambrose, is something exhausted soldiers can do. Averaging over thirty miles a day, Greene's
whole army made it to the Dan River ferries where his quartermaster
had collected six boats to use in the crossing—this thanks to a survey
of boats that Greene had earlier ordered done. With these boats,
Greene crossed the river to safety, although he did not realize it at the
time and was prepared to continue to retreat beyond the Banister
River. On 14 February, Greene was making such preparations to
retreat further, writing Williams that he had not had four hours sleep
since he had spent time with Williams four days earlier. Cornwallis
chose not to continue the pursuit, however, and the Southern army
was saved.

While the story of the retreat is remarkable, even more remarkable is
the fact that Greene, less than a week after eluding Cornwallis on
this great retreat, sent parts of his army back across the Dan into
Virginia. Let me give you the chronology. Greene and his army
crossed the Dan on 13 February at Irwin's and Boyd's ferries, on 19
February, elements of his army re-cross the Dan and begin pursuit of

Cornwallis, and on 25 February, those advance forces overtake and defeat a loyalist militia force at an engagement called Pyle's Massacre. Less than three weeks later, Nathanael Greene moves to a position to challenge Cornwallis at Guilford Court House, and in essence threw down the gauntlet. Here, to refer to the image Greene used, the crab reversed its course, and began scuttling forward to probe and harass and finally to cripple Cornwallis' army in the battle of Guilford Court House.

It can be said, then, that in roughly six weeks an under-manned, ill-equipped, demoralized army reversed America's fortunes and recaptured a large part of the South. Makes crossing the Delaware on Christmas eve seem like child's play by comparison, doesn't it.

What you have begun here with the Retreat to the Dan Memorial is laudable. I applaud you and fervently wish that you will continue to build on this beginning until the crossing of the Dan receives the kind of recognition that it deserves. This achievement by Nathanael Greene and his army was one of the most important episodes in our nation's history and deserves to be remembered as such.

*Note:* Dr. Dennis Conrad, Editor of the *Nathanael Greene Papers* at the Rhode Island Historical Society, delivered this address in South Boston, Virginia, on the occasion of a memorial dedicated by the Berryman Green Chapter of the National Society of the Daughters of the American Revolution to Nathanael Greene's crossing of the Dan River in February 1781.

# The Prizery:
# Its Journey Into the Past

*SAR Magazine* 2006

The echo of Compatriot Douglas Powell's footsteps permeated the silence of the stairwell in The Prizery—a century old abandoned tobacco factory in South Boston, Virginia. As he entered a vast and vacant upstairs room, he envisioned times gone by when tobacco was king and the leaves were "prized" or pressed layer by layer in hogshead barrels for later shipment.

Douglas Powell and Barbara Bass observing Boyd's Ferry site from the third floor window of The Prizery in South Boston. (The permanent exhibit telling the story will surround this window.)

The smells and sounds of ongoing renovations reminded Powell that The Prizery's past was now being transformed into a community, fine arts, and welcome center, complete with banquet hall and theater.

As Powell, a member of the Dan River Chapter of the Virginia Society SAR, surveyed the room, he turned and noticed a window behind him. The parking lot below was not what suddenly captured his attention. It was the perfect view of Boyd's ferry site.

That ferry site, along with Irwin's ferry four miles upstream, was used by Nathanael Greene's army as his men escaped the clutches of Cornwallis' veteran British troops in the Race to the Dan during the winter of 1781. Like the evacuation of Dunkirk in World War II, boats were gathered together to transport Greene's army across the river on February 13-14. When Cornwallis arrived, Nathanael Greene's troops were safe on the other side of the river with all the boats. All Cornwallis could do was watch the celebration.

An aerial veiw of the site for Boyd's Ferry

Greene's crossing of the Dan River was not just another retreat in the face of a superior enemy. It rescued the American Revolution from certain disaster, and also set the stage for the Battle of Guilford Courthouse followed by the surrender at Yorktown.

It was this crossing of the river that Compatriot Powell thought of when he gazed out the window. He envisioned an exhibit that would tell General Greene's story and what happened beyond the tree line on the banks of the Dan River over 200 years ago.

Powell, also a board member of the Halifax County Historical Society, one of the user groups at The Prizery, began promoting his idea. Through the leadership of President Barbara Bass, the Society made floor space available for the exhibit and appointed Compatriot Powell to chair a committee to make it happen. Important community leaders, such as South Boston's Town Manager, Colonel Ted

Daniel, as well as retired judge and former Virginia House of Delegates member Frank Slayton have joined the effort.

Work on the exhibit began in 2004, with volunteers conducting research and Dr. Ralph Wileman, University of North Carolina professor emeritus, developing a design. Virginia's 5th District Congressman Virgil Goode assisted the group in securing an initial $20,000 planning grant. Further funding will be needed to complete the project in time for America's 400th Anniversary at Jamestown in 2007.

When completed, the exhibit will highlight the major military leaders and battles in the Southern Campaign of the American Revolution, especially the events involved in Greene's retreat across the Carolinas and his crossing of the Dan River.

A timeline of the retreat and a wall mural of the Crossing will also greet visitors. A large interactive wall map will offer audio descriptions of selected events as re-enactors portray the voices of Cornwallis, Nathanael Greene, and others.

At the end of the exhibit tour, visitors will stand where Douglas Powell stood alone that day at the top of the stairs and saw the ferry site. Because of private property restrictions, and lack of accessibility, the site has never been available for the general public to visit or see. Now, for the first time, the Boyd's Ferry location can be viewed from The Prizery's third floor vantage point. Also, at the window a video presentation will detail the movement of men and supplies across the river.

According to President Barbara Bass, with the exhibit's completion, the Halifax County Historical Society will host a resource room to allow guests to research local history and that related to Greene's Southern Campaign. Future plans include a model of a boat used by Greene's troops as they crossed the river and an artist's rendition of Greene crossing the Dan.

Also in the early stages of development are living history and lecture series presentations for next year's commemoration of Greene's Crossing. This effort will complement the Lighting Freedom's Flame initiative, sponsored by the National Park Service, which will emphasize the 225th Anniversary of the American Revolution.

The goal of the exhibit and these related activities is not just to teach a history lesson filled with names and dates and battle descriptions. Visitors will gain an appreciation of Greene's magnificent maneuvers throughout the South during that war and understand the significance that the crossing of the Dan River by Greene's army had on the outcome of the American Revolution.

Although the ferry site below The Prizery doesn't tell the whole story, Historical Society President Barbara Bass says, "The window will honor the memory of local historian Carroll Headspeth, whose book *The Retreat to the Dan* was published in 1974 for the American Bicentennial."

Headspeth kept the story alive and reminded readers of its importance. He wrote, "For it was General Nathanael Greene's successful retreat and crossing of the Dan that contributed greatly to the final victory at Yorktown."

Many visitors are expected to look through that window and see for the first time the very spot where a pivotal turning point of the Revolution took place. As they gaze outwardly, toward the Dan River, visitors will hear in their minds the echo of sounds made over 200 years ago—sounds of struggling men, marching 40 miles the last 16 hours toward the Dan, half-starved and miserably cold, leaving their bloody footprints on the ground. Sounds of thrashing water as horses and men hurry to cross the wide expanse of the rapidly moving and flooded Dan River.

They will imagine, too, the debilitated and exhausted men of Greene's army raising their voices in strained huzzahs as the last man crossed the river.

As their imaginations soar, visitors may also smell the gunpowder from distant volleys of musketry firing in the shadow of recoiling cannons. Ghostly images of men, known by few, may appear as breathless warriors lying on frozen fields of far away battles, their faces fixed in stony silence from having sacrificed themselves for freedom's sake.

As that happens, the Crossing of the Dan exhibit at South Boston, Virginia, with the Headspeth Window facing the river, will allow the light of liberty to brighten hearts anew.

The Prizery with the third floor Headspeth window facing Boyd's ferry site.

General Greene, reviewing his army, at length safely enjoying wholesome and abundant supplies of food in the rich and friendly county of Halifax, bestowed upon all his commendation . . .

—Light-Horse Harry Lee
1812 edition of his *Memoirs*

The present moment is big with the most important consequences, & requires the greatest and most spirited exertions.

> —Nathanael Greene to Patrick Henry, dated February 10, 1781, from Guilford Courthouse as Greene's army prepared for the race to the Dan River near South Boston, Virginia.

# Crossing of the Dan
## 225th Anniversary Celebration
*Evince* Magazine, 2006

The best kept secret of Southside Virginia happened 225 years ago this February right in our own backyard. Now the extraordinary event will be celebrated in South Boston on February 10-11th.

Over two centuries ago, the future of the American Revolution hung like a slender thread on the rain swollen waters of the Dan River, from Dix's Ferry (which was located behind what is now Danville's airport) to Irvins' and Boyd's ferries near South Boston.

The Dan River was the finish line for a race unparalleled in American history. The race had begun 200 miles further south, when an American army headed North in an attempt to avoid capture by a far superior British force intent on subduing the Southern Colonies and thus crushing the War for Independence.

It was a frightening drama played out before a fledgling nation. The struggling American Colonists were hemmed in. Mountains blocked a Westward escape. British troops were ensconced in the North in New York. The British Navy lay menacingly off the East coast. And all the while, Cornwallis with his elite British troops ravaged the South.

The eyes of the whole nation focused on a bedraggled Southern army cobbled together by General Nathanael Greene. They alone stood between the surrender of the Southern Colonies and the subsequent defeat of Washington's army through the back door.

Cornwallis headed after Greene like a rabid fox in a hen house — anticipating Greene's now famous strategic retreat, which actually became maneuvers enticing Cornwallis across North Carolina toward Virginia, far away from his British supply lines and any reinforcements.

The winter of 1781 was bitterly cold. Greene's army was reduced almost to rags, had little food, and only a few blankets. Many men had no shoes. Rain, snow, and probably sleet hampered horses, wagons, and men as they mired up in the slush of the muddy red clay. At night, the slush froze, creating rutted ice-encrusted roads capable of shredding human flesh, hobbling horses, and dismembering both cannon and wagons.

Greene's army, shivering and starving, marched non-stop, day and night. Short on everything but courage, they valiantly willed themselves to the Dan River just ahead of the British.

On February 13-14, 1781, Greene's army crossed that engorged river on waiting boats, leaving Cornwallis' army stranded on the other side with no way to cross.

Cornwallis was forced to retreat. Greene's troops, now resupplied and reinforced, followed. In perhaps the most costly and bloodiest battle of the Revolution, the British and the Americans confronted one another at Guilford Courthouse (now in Greensboro). Cornwallis' troops were so mauled that they sought refuge in Wilmington and then advanced to Yorktown, where he surrendered.

Had Greene's army not won the Race to the Dan River, Guilford and Yorktown would not have happened. General Greene's brilliance as a strategist had not only saved his army, but effectively had saved the American Revolution. To General Washington, Greene wrote a heart-rending dispatch on February 15, 1781. Recounting the previous day's crossing of the Dan River, his words are poignant reminders of the sacrifices of his army: "The miserable situation of the troops for want of clothing had rendered the march the most painful imaginable, several hundreds of the soldiers tracking the ground with their bloody feet."

Those footprints have been long erased by the ravages of time, but they are not forgotten. When Nathanael Greene's Crossing is celebrated on February 10-11, 2006, it will be the largest gathering to recognize the event since Greene's army was there 225 years ago. Explaining the significance of this momentous anniversary of

Greene's Crossing to the region, Barbara Bass, Vice-Regent of the Berryman Green Chapter of the Daughters of the American Revolution, and President of the Halifax County Historical Society, says, "This story has been in the wings waiting to take center stage for 225 years and now it will happen. It is our responsibility to preserve history and to share it with others."

Acknowledging that few people know about Greene's Crossing of the Dan, Dan Shaw, Coordinator for the Crossing Events, echoes her sentiments. "It is our goal to change this story of uncommon knowledge into a proud heritage of common knowledge. Our schools should be teaching it."

To this end, Douglas Powell, a member of the local Dan River Chapter of the Sons of the American Revolution and the Chairman of the Crossing of the Dan Exhibit Committee, says, "The goals of the two-day event are to provide an enjoyable experience for those attending, to share the story of our region's part in this most important historical event, to help educate the young about local history, and to call attention and gain support for the plans to create a permanent exhibit."

Think of it this way. When you come to this anniversary celebration you will walk where Greene's soldiers walked and where their bloody footprints, each one a small step for our country, remain an invisible but large step for the liberty that they, and others like them, bought so dearly.

They gave us a Republic, but only by remembering will we keep it.

The Army being in great distress for want of a number of bags, to transport the Meal for the Troops, Casks being found very inconvenient, . . . The Inhabitants of Halifax County are therefore desir'd to furnish for the use of the public [i.e., the army] immediately, three hundred to be brought to the Army as soon as possible. The Army cannot get a supply in any other way . . .

—Nathanael Greene to
Inhabitants of Halifax County
February 16, 1781

# Remarks at the Memorial Service
## February 11, 2006
## South Boston, Virginia
## The 225th Anniversary of Greene's
## Crossing of the Dan River

I bring you greetings from the Dan River Chapter of the Sons of the American Revolution. We have come here to pay homage to our ancestors who fought in the Southern Campaign of that war. One of my ancestors fought at the Battle of Stono during the Siege of Charleston; his father shoed horses and repaired guns for General Nathanael Greene's men after they crossed the Dan River.

Today though, we are assembled near this river — perhaps the largest gathering of Patriots to celebrate this event since Greene's army was actually here 225 years ago.

But I have also come here alone. One cold February day in the year 2000 near the anniversary of Greene's Crossing, I stood on the banks of this river. For a few moments I stared across the water into the distant horizon as snow drifted down around me. As my mind wandered back across the centuries, I thought I saw that army march the long march during one of the worse winters on record.

Their demeanor was haggard, but their eyes shone like resolute beacons. Their dress was ragged, but I sensed they were knit together as one with the golden cord of freedom. Their stomachs were hungry, but their hearts were full, pulsating with patriotism. Their steps were heavy, made more painful by the hard frozen ground beneath their feet. Like dead men walking, they willed themselves onward — staggering through the dark of night — gasping with every breath of bitterly cold air.

But when they reached the river, I thought I saw those faltering footsteps, though small steps for a man, come alive and become a giant leap for liberty as they crossed to the other side. This was their moment of magnificence. They not only saved themselves, but they rescued the Revolution once again.

It is ironic that at this very hour the 2006 Winter Olympic Games are taking place. There will be races and competitions for gold and glory, but none of those will compare with the Race to the Dan.

Those soldiers who marched with General Greene were no summer Soldiers or sunshine Patriots. Yet, they received no medals—no garlands of glory came their way. But what they did that day they crossed the Dan made them every man a hero.

We stand here today where they stood—beside the ghostly remnants of those bloody footprints they left upon the ground—a constant reminder that the price of freedom is never cheap, but is paid for with eternal vigilance and sacrifice.

Yes, they gave us a Republic, but they first gave us the gift of themselves that we might follow in their footsteps.

May God bless the sacred memory of General Greene and his band of brothers, and may God bless this country we love, the United States of America.

Larry G. Aaron  
Past President and Founder  
Dan River Chapter, VA Society, SAR

# Boyd's Ferry Today

For 225 years—every day, every night—the Dan River has flowed nonstop past the site of Greene's Crossing. The town of South Boston has grown around the site, now located near the railroad bridge that crosses the river. Today, trains cross the river in seconds in contrast to Greene's Army, which took several hours in bitterly cold weather as they outraced Cornwallis' British troops to the Dan.

Had it not been for Greene's successful crossing of the river in February 1781 at Boyd's and Irwin's ferries, there might not have been an America and with it the development of enterprise and industry like the railroads that haul coal and freight to distant places. The trains cross the river constantly and the river moves silently below them, joining past and future together.

A snowy day in February near the Boyd's Ferry site where the railroad bridge crosses the Dan River. The site remains much as it was when General Greene's army crossed the river in 1781.

There appear to be no traces of the ferry today, and the forested landscape along the river's edge certainly has changed. To the right of Boyd's Ferry stretches the main bridge which feeds off Route 58 and takes vehicles into South Boston. The Prizery, an old tobacco processing factory, looks down upon the crossing site from atop the embankment directly beyond it.

Despite any remaining evidence of a ferry, on a cold snowy day in winter one can still imagine Greene's army marching through the trees where Route 58 now runs and the ferry flat boats crisscrossing the river taking Greene's army to the other side. Boyd's and Irwin's ferries, though gone now, obliterated by the ravages of time and made obsolete by modern means of transportation, forever hold a place in American history for their role in saving Greene's army and securing the American Revolution.

This Virginia Historical Marker is located in South Boston near Boyd's Ferry, site of the crossing of 1781.

Boyd's Ferry site as it appeared in February 2000. Snow still lies on the far side of the river bank.

This covered bridge built in 1854 across the Dan River meant the end of Boyd's Ferry and a new beginning.

Crossing of the Dan memorial dedicated February 13, 1999, South Boston, Virginia, by the Berryman Green Chapter of the NSDAR.

Providence has blessed the American Arms . . .
with more success than we had reason to expect
in our miserable situation.

— General Greene to Congress
January 31, 1781

# Part III
## Resource Materials

General References
Magazine/Journal Articles
Ph.D. Dissertations
Master's Theses
Books for Young People
Annotated Online Sources
Movies and DVDs
Music (CDs)

Greene is however entitled to great praise for his wonderful exertions; the more he is beaten, the further he advances in the end. He has been indefatigable in collecting troops and leading them to be defeated.

—From the diary of a British
officer quoted in Hugh F. Rankin's
*Greene and Cornwallis: The
Campaign in the Carolinas*.

# Resource Materials

This listing is intended to provide help for those researching the American Revolution and in particular the Race to the Dan and the Southern Campaign. However, no bibliography can be complete because new books and research materials are constantly being published. Furthermore, although extensive, this bibliography is not exhaustive concerning available publications.

The sources listed also consist of new or recent materials, as well those which are out of print, in which case they may be found in only rare manuscript rooms of major university libraries, at rare booksellers, or in private libraries.

These references do not include all available collected papers, and other materials at state archives, state libraries and university libraries of the southern states of Virginia, North and South Carolina, and Georgia. Also very valuable are pension applications of Revolutionary War veterans available through the National Archives of the United States. These documents contain a plethora of information in addition to what has been included in this bibliography.

Diaries and letters available from participants in the war are also great sources as are court documents in specific localities. Although some local materials are listed in this bibliography, many more materials can be found through local libraries, historical and genealogical societies, museums, and other organizations in a particular locality where events in the Southern Campaign took place. Local historians are usually well-versed in nearby events.

A good source for maps is the Library of Congress. Also, searching the Library of Congress as well as the libraries of universities through their online Internet catalogues may reveal microfilm or books available by interlibrary loan. The Internet sources given here are just a few of the many available on the Revolutionary War, but these will provide links to others. Even now the entire text of some of the sources in this reference listing are available on the Internet.

Re-enactment group sites are sources of information and music. Online bookstores including http://www.amazon.com, http://www.abebooks.com and http://www.ebay.com (the online auction site) have new and used books.

## *General References*

*A Preliminary Guide to Pre-1904 Records in the Virginia State Library and Archives*. Richmond, VA: Virginia State Library and Archives, 1994.

Abbazia, Patrick. *Nathanael Greene: Commander of the American Continental Army in the South*. Charlottesville, VA: SamHar Press, 1976.

Abbott, W. W., ed. *The Papers of George Washington,* Colonial Series. Vol. I. Charlottesville: University Press of Virginia, 1983.

Abercrombie, Janice L. and Richard L. Slatten, comp. *Virginia Revolutionary "Publick" Claims*. 3 vols. Athens, GA: Iberian Publishing Co., 1992.

Adams, Randolph G. *Political Ideas of the American Revolution*. Barnes and Noble, 1958.

Agniel, Lucien. *The Late Affair Has Almost Broke My Heart: The American Revolution in the South 1780-1781*. Riverside, CT: Chatham, 1972.

_____. *Rebels Victorious: The American Revolution in the South, 1780-1781*. New York: Ballatine Books, 1975.

Alden, John Richard. *A History of the American Revolution*. New York: Knopf, 1969.

_____. *The American Revolution, 1775-1783*. New York: Harper and Row, 1962.

_____. *The South in the American Revolution, 1763-1789*. Baton Rouge: Louisiana State University Press, 1957.

_____. *George Washington, a Biography*. Baton Rouge: Louisiana State University Press, 1984.

Alexander, Holmes M. *Washington and Lee: A Study in the Will to Win*. Boston: Western Islands, 1966.

Allaire, Anthony. *Diary of Lieut. Anthony Alliare*. New York: Arno, 1968 [Originally published in 1881. Lt. Alliare was with Ferguson's Corps at King's Mountain].

Allen, Edward M. *LaFayette's Second Expedition to Virginia 1781*. Baltimore, MD: J. Murphy, 1891.

Andrews, Charles. M. and Frances G. Davenport, eds. *Guide to the Manuscript Materials for the History of the United States to 1783, in the British Museum, in Minor London Archives, and in the Libraries of Oxford and Cambridge*. Washington, DC: 1908.

_____, ed. *Guide to the Materials for American History, to 1783, in the Public Record Office of Great Britain*, 2 vols. Washington, DC, 1912-1914.

_____. *The Colonial Background of the American Revolution*. New Haven, Yale University Press, 1931.

Andrist, Ralph K., ed. *George Washington: A Biography in His Own Words*. New York: *Newsweek*, 1972.

Army War College Historical Section. *Historical Statements Concerning the Battle of Kings' Mountain and the Battle of the Cowpens, South Carolina*. Washington, DC: GPO, 1928.

Arthur, Robert. *The End of a Revolution*. New York: Vantage Press, 1965.

Atwood, Rodney. *The Hessians: Mercenaries from Hessen-Kassel in the American Revolution*. Cambridge, England: Cambridge University Press, 1980.

Ayling, Stanley E. *The Elder Pitt, Earl of Chatham*. New York: D. Mckay, 1976.

Babits, Lawrence E. *A Devil of a Whipping: The Battle of Cowpens*. Chapel Hill: The University of North Carolina Press, 1998.

_____. *Cowpens Battlefield: A Walking Guide*. Johnson City, TN: The Overmountain Press, 1993.

_____. *Southern Campaigns*. Eastern National, 2002.

Bailyn, Bernard. *Faces of Revolution: Personalities and Themes in the Struggle for American Independence*. New York: Knopf, 1990.

_____. *The Ideological Origins of the American Revolution*. Cambridge, MA: Harvard University Press, 1967.

Baker, Thomas E. *Another Such Victory*. Eastern Acorn Press, Eastern National Park and Monument Association, 1981.

Bancroft, George. *History of the United States*. Vol. IX. Boston: Little Brown, 1866.

Barbour, R. L. *South Carolina's Revolutionary War Battlefields: A Tour Guide*. Gretna, LA: Pelican Publishing, 2002.

Barefoot, Daniel. *Touring North Carolina's Revolutionary War Sites*. Winston-Salem: John FBlair Publishing, 1998.

_____. *Touring South Carolina's Revolutionary War Sites*, Winston-Salem: John FBlair Publishing, 1999.

Bass, Robert D. *Ninety-Six, The Struggle for the South Carolina Back Country.* Orangeburg, SC: Sandlapper Publishing Co., 1978.

_____. *Swamp Fox: the Life and Campaigns of General Francis Marion.* New York: Henry Holt, 1959.

_____. *The Green Dragoon: The Lives of Banastre Tarleton and Mary Robinson.* New York: Henry Holt, 1957.

_____. *Gamecock: The Life and Campaigns of Thomas Sumter* New York: Holt, Rinehart andWinston, 1951.

Bearss, Edwin C. *Battle of Cowpens: A Documented Narrative.* Johnson City, TN: The Overmountain Press, 1996.

Beatson, Robert. *Naval and Military Memoirs of Great Britain from 1727-1783.* Vol. VI. Boston: Gregg Press, 1972.

Becker, Carl L. *The Declaration of Independence.* New York: Knopf, 1942.

Belcher, Henry. *First American Civil War.* 2 vols. London: 1911.

Bemis, Samuel F. *The Diplomacy of the American Revolution.* New York: D. Appleton-Century, 1935.

Bennett, Charles E. and Donald R. Lennon. *A Quest for Glory: Major General Robert Howe and the American Revolution.* Chapel Hill: University of North Carolina Press, 1991.

Berken, Carol. *Revolutionary Mothers: Women in the Struggle for America's Independence.* New York: Knopf, 2005.

Billias, George Athan. *George Washington's Generals*. New York: William Morrow, 1964.

_____, ed. *The American Revolution: How Revolutionary Was It?* New York: Holt, Rinehart, Winston, 1965.

Blanco, Richard L., ed. *The American Revolution, 1775-1783*. New York: Garland, 1993.

Blulm, Col. Raymond K., Jr. *U. S. Army: A Complete History*. Arlington: The Army Historical Foundation, 2004.

Boatner, Mark M. III. *Encyclopedia of the American Revolution*. New York: David McKay Co., 1966.

_____. *Landmarks of the Revolution: People and Places Vital to the Quest for Independence*. Harrisburg: Stackpole, 1992.

Boddie, William Willis. *Traditions of the Swamp Fox: Williams W. Boddie's Francis Marion*. Spartanburg, SC: Reprint Co., 2000.

Bolton, Charles K. *The Private Soldier Under Washington*. Kennikat, 1964.

Bonwick, Colin. *The American Revolution*. Charlottesville: University Press of Virginia, 1991.

Boorstin, Daniel J. *The Americans: The Colonial Experience*. New York: Vintage, 1958.

Bowler, Arthur. *Logistics and the Failure of the British Army in America, 1775-1783*. Princeton, NJ: Princeton University Press, 1975.

Bowman, Allen. *The Morale of the American Revolutionary Army*. Washington, DC: American Council on Public Affairs, 1943.

Boyd, Julian P., ed. *The Papers of Thomas Jefferson*. Vol. VI. October 1780-February 1781. Princeton, NJ: Princeton University Press, 1951.

_____. *The Papers of Thomas Jefferson*. Vol. V. February 1781-May 1781. Princeton, NJ: Princeton University Press, 1952.

Boyd, Thomas. *Light-Horse Harry Lee*. New York: C. Scribner's Sons, 1931.

Bracey, Susan. *Life by the Roaring Roanoke: A History of Mecklenberg County, Virginia*. Mecklenberg County Bicentennial Commission, 1977.

Bridenbaugh, Carl. *The Spirit of 76*. New York: Oxford, 1975.

Brooke, John. *King George III*. London: Constable, 1972.

Brown, Gerald S. *The American Secretary*. Ann Arbor: University of Michigan, 1963.

Brown, Wallace. *The Good Americans: The Loyalists in the American Revolution*. New York: Morrow, 1969.

_____. *The King's Friends*. Providence, RI: Brown University, 1965.

Brumell, Stephen. *Redcoats: The British Soldier and War in the Americas, 1755-1763*. New York: Cambridge, 2002.

Buchanan, John. *The Road to Guilford Courthouse: The American Revolution in the Carolinas*. New York: John Wiley and Sons, Inc., 1997.

Burgess, Louis A. *Virginia Soldiers of 1776*. Richmond, Virginia: Richmond Press, 1927.

Caldwell, Charles. *Memoirs of the Life and Campaigns of the Honorable Nathaniel [sic] Greene, Major General in the Army of the United States, and Commander of the Southern Department, in the War of the Revolution*. Philadelphia: Robert and Thomas Desilver, 1819.

Callahan, North. *Daniel Morgan: Ranger of the Revolution*. Holt, Reinhart, Winston, 1961.

_____. *George Washington, Soldier and Man*. New York: Morrow, 1972.

Calloway, Colin G. *The American Revolution in Indian Country: Crisis and Diversity in Native American Communities*. New York: Cambridge University Press, 1995.

Cannon, Richard. *Historical Records of the British Army; comprising the history of every regiment in His Majesty's service*. London: 1834-1850.

Carnes, Mark C. and John A. Garraty. *Mapping America's Past: A Historical Atlas*. New York: Henry Holt, 1996.

Cappon, Lester J. *The Atlas of Early American History: The Revolutionary Era, 1760-1790*. Princeton, NJ: Princeton University Press, 1976.

Carrington, Henry B. *Battles of the American Revolution; Battle Maps and Charts of The American Revolution*, (combined edition of *Battles of the American Revolution, 1887*, and *Battle Maps and Charts of the American Revolution, 1881*). New York: The New York Times and Arno Press, 1974.

Carrington, Henry B. *Battles of the American Revolution, 1775-1781. Historical and Military Criticism, with Topographical Illustration*. New York: A. S. Barnes & Co., 1871, 1876.

Caruthers, E. W. *Interesting Revolutionary Incidents; and Sketches of Character, Chiefly in the "Old North State."* Philadelphia: Hayes & Zell, 1856.

Cashin, Edward J. *The King's Ranger: Thomas Brown and the American Revolution on the Southern Frontier.* Athens, GA: University of Georgia Press, 1989.

Catton Bruce and William B. Catton. *The Bold and Magnificent Dream: America's Founding Years 1492-1815.* New York: Doubleday, 1978.

Chambers, John Whiteclay II, editor-in-chief. *The Oxford Companion to American Military History.* New York: Oxford University Press, 1999.

Channing, Edward. *History of the United States.* New York: 1905-1912.

Chastellux, Marquis de. *Travels in North America in the Years 1780, 1781, and 1782.* Edited by Howard C. Rice. Chapel Hill: University of North Carolina Press, 1963.

Chidsey, Donald B. *The War in the South: The Carolinas and Georgia in the American Revolution: An Informal History.* New York: Crown, 1969.

Christie, I. R. *Crisis of Empire: Great Britain and The American Colonies, 1754-1783.* New York: W. W. Norton, 1966.

Church, Randolph W. *Virginia Legislative Petitions, Bibliography, Calendar, and Abstracts from Original Sources, 6 May 1776 – 21 June 1782.* Richmond: Virginia State Library, 1984.

Churchill, Winston S. *The Age of Revolution.* New York: Dodd, Mead, 1957.

Clark, Walter, ed. *The State Records of North Carolina*. 16 vols. Winston Salem and Goldsboro, NC: 1895-1906.

Clements, Maud Carter, *The History of Pittsylvania County, Virginia*. Lynchburg: J. PBell Company, 1929; reprinted by the Pittsylvania County Historical Society, 1988.

Clinton, Sir Henry. *The American Rebellion: Sir Henry Clinton's Narrative of His Campaigns, 1775-1782*. Edited by William B. Wilcox. New Haven, CT: Yale University Press, 1954.

Coakley, Robert W. and Stetson Conn. *The War of the American Revolution: Narrative, Chronology, and Bibliography*. Washington, DC: U.S. Army Center of Military History, 1975.

Coffin, Charles C. *Boys of '76: A History of the Battles of the Revolution*. Nork York: Harper, 1876.

Coleman, Kenneth. *The American Revolution in Georgia, 1763-1789*. Athens, GA: University of Georgia Press, 1958.

Commanger, Henry Steele and Richard B. Morris. *The Spirit of Seventy-Six, The Story of the American Revolution as Told by its Participants*. 2 vols. Edison, NJ: Castle Books, 1958.

Compton, Spurgeon and Headspeth, W. Carroll. *The Retreat to the Dan*. South Boston, VA: South Boston News, 1974.

Conrad. Dennis M., ed. et als. *The Papers of General Nathanael Greene*, Vol. VIII, 30 March-10 July 1781. Chapel Hill: The University of North Carolina Press, 1995.

Conway, Stephen. *The War of American Independence 1775-1783*. New York, St. Martin's Press, 1995.

Cook, Don. *The Long Fuse: How England Lost the American Colonies, 1760-1785*. New York: Atlantic Monthly Press, 1995.

Cornwallis, Charles. *An Answer to that Part of the Narrative of Lieutenant-Gen. Sir Henry Clinton, K.B. Which Relates to the Conduct of Lieutenant-Gen. Earl Cornwallis During the Campaign in North America in the Year 1781.* London: Debrett, 1783.

Corwin, Edward S. *French Policy and the American Alliance of 1778.* Princeton: 1916.

Countryman, Edward. *The American Revolution.* New York: Hill and Wang, 1985.

Coupland, R. *The American Revolution and the British Empire.* New York: Russell and Russell, 1965.

Crews, C. Daniel. *Through Fiery Trials: The Revolutionary War and the Moravians.* Winston-Salem, NC: Moravian Archives, 1996.

Crow, Jeffrey J. *A Chronicle of North Carolina during the American Revolution 1768 – 1789.* Raleigh: Division of Archives and History, North Carolina Department of Cultural Resources, 1997 reprint of 1975 edition.

Crow, Jeffrey J., and Larry E. Tise, eds. *The Southern Experience in the American Revolution.* Chapel Hill: University of North Carolina Press, 1978.

Crozier, W. A. *The Virginia Colonial Militia.* Baltimore: Genealogical Publishing Company, 1982.

Cumming, William P. and Hugh Rankin. *The Fate of a Nation: The American Revolution through Contemporary Eyes.* London: Phaidon, 1975.

Curtis, Edward E. *The Organization of the British Army in the American Revolution.* New York: AMS Press, 1969.

Dann, John C., ed. *The Revolution Remembered: Eyewitness Accounts Of The War For Independence*. Chicago: University of Chicago Press, 1980.

Daves, Edward Graham. *Maryland and North Carolina in the Campaign of 1780-1781; With a Preliminary Notice of the Earlier Battles of the Revolution, in which the Troops of the Two States Won Distinction*. Baltimore: J. Murphy & Co., 1893.

Davidson, Chalmers Gaston. *Piedmont Partisan: The Life and Times of Brigadier General William Lee Davidson*. Davidson, NC: Davidson College, 1951.

Davie, William R. *Revolutionary War Sketches of William R. Davie*. Blackwell P. Robinson, ed. Raleigh: North Carolina Division of Archives and History, 1976.

Davis, Burke. *The Campaign That Won America: The Story of Yorktown*. Acorn Press, Eastern National Monument Association, 1970.

_____. *The Cowpens-Guilford Courthouse Campaign*. Philadelphia: J. B. Lippincott Co., 1962.

Davis, Chester S. *Moravians in Europe and America 1415-1865*. Winston-Salem, NC: Wachovia Historical Society, 2000.

Dederer, John M. *Making Bricks Without Straw: Nathanael Greene's Southern Campaigns and Mao Tse-Tung's Mobile War*. Manhattan, Kansas: Sunflower University, 1983.

Deerin, James B. *The Militia in the Revolutionary War*. Washington, DC: Historical Society of Militia & National Guard, 1976.

DeMond, Robert O. *The Loyalists in North Carolina During the Revolution*. Durham, NC: Duke University Press, 1958.

Dhohla, Johann C. *A Hessian Diary of the American Revolution.* University of Oklahoma, 1990.

Dobein, James W. *A Sketch of the Life of Brig. Gen. Francis Marion, and a History of his Brigade.* Charleston, SC: 1821.

Donne, W. B. *Correspondence of George III with Lord North.* 2 vols. London: 1867.

Donoughue, Bernard. *British Politics and the American Revolution.* New York: Macmillan, 1964.

Dorman, John Frederick. *Virginia Revolutionary War State Pensions.* EasleySC: Southern Historical Press, 1982.

Draper, Lyman Copeland. *King's Mountain and Its Heroes: History of the Battle of King's Mountain, October 7th, 1780 and the Events Which Led to It.* Cincinnati: Peter G. Thomson, 1881.

Draper, Theodore. *A Struggle for Power: The American Revolution.* New York: Time Books/Random House, 1996.

Drayton, John. *Memoirs of the American Revolution, & c., as relating to the State of South Carolina.* Charleston: 1821.

Draper, Theodore. *A Struggle for Power: The American Revolution.* New York: Times Books, 1976.

Driver, Carl S. *John Sevier.* Chapel Hill: University Press of North Carolina, 1932.

Droughton, Margaret and Sally Elder Welch., comp. *North Carolina Biographical Sketches of Soldiers and Patriots in the Battle of Guilford Courthouse March 15, 1781.* Greensboro, NC: The Rachel Caldwell Chapter NC DAR, 1959.

Duffy, Christopher. *The Military Experience in the Age of Reason.* NY: Atheneum, 1988.

Dupuy, R. Ernest and Dupuy, Trevor N. *The Compact History of the Revolutionary War*. New York, Hawthorn Books, 1963.

Dupuy, Trevor N. *People and Events of the American Revolution*. R. R. Bowker, 1974.

Eanes, Greg. *Tarleton's Southside Raid: Prelude to Yorktown*. Burkeville, VA: E & H Publishing Company, 2002.

Eckenrode, H. J. *List of Colonial Soldiers of Virginia (Special Report of the Department of Archives and History for 1913)*. Baltimore: Genealogical Publishing CompanyInc., 1978.

_____. *The Revolution in Virginia*. Hamden, CT: Archon Books, 1964.

Edgar, Walter B. *Partisans and Redcoats: The Southern Campaign that Turned the Tide of the American Revolution*. New York: William Morrow, 2001.

Eller, Ernest McNeill. *Chesapeake Bay in the American Revolution*. Centreville, MD: Tidewater Publishers, 1981.

Ellet, E. E. *Domestic History of the American Revolution*. New York: Baker and Scribner, 1850.

Ellis, Joseph J. *His Excellency: George Washington*. New York: Knopf, 2004.

Evans, A. W. W. *Memoirs of Kuscuizko: Poland's Hero and Patriot*. New York: Society of the Cincinnati, 1883.

Ewald, Johann. *Diary of the American War: A Hessian Journal*. Joseph P. Trustin, translator and ed. New Haven: Yale University Press, 1979.

Fanning, David. *The Narrative of Colonel David Fanning (A Tory in the Revolutionary War) Giving an Account of His Adventures in North Carolina from 1775-1783.* New York: Joseph Sabin, 1865.

Faragher, John M., ed. *The Encyclopedia of Colonial and Revolutionary America.* New York: Facts on File, 1990.

Ferling, John, ed. *The World Turned Upside Down: The American Victory in the War of Independence.* New York: Greenwood Press, 1988.

Fiske, John. *The American Revolution.* Boston: Houghton Mifflin, 1891.

Fisher, Sydney G. *The Struggle for American Independence.* 2 vols. Philadelphia: 1908.

Fitzpatrick, John. *The Writings of George Washington, from the Original Manuscript Sources, 1745-1799.* 39 Vols. Washington, DC: United States Government Printing Office, 1931-1944.

Fleming, Thomas. *Liberty! The American Revolution.* New York: Viking Penguin, 1997.

Fleming, Thomas J. *Downright Fighting: The Story of Cowpens—The Official National Park Handbook.* Washington, DC: Division of Publications: National Park Service, United States Department of the Interior, 1988.

Flood, Charles Bracelen. *Rise, And Fight Again: Perilous Times Along the Road to Independence.* New York: Dodd, Mead, 1976.

Ford, Paul L. *The Works of Thomas Jefferson.* 12 Vols. New York and London: G. P. Putnam's Sons, 1904-1905.

Ford, Washington E. *British Officers Serving in the American Revolution 1774-1783*. Brooklyn, NY: Historical Printing Club, 1897.

Fortescue, J. W. *History of the British Army*. 10 vols. London: 1899-1920.

Flexnor, James Thomas. *George Washington in the American Revolution, 1775-1783*. Boston: Little, Brown, 1967.

Fowler, Jr., William M. *Rebels Under Sail: The American Navy During the Revolution*. New York: Charles Scribner's Sons, 1976.

Freeman, Douglas Southall. *George Washington: Leader of the Revolution*. 7 vols. New York: Schribner, 1951.

Frey, Sylvia R. *The British Soldier in America*. Austin, TX: University of Texas Press, 1981.

Fries, Adelaide L. *Records of the Moravians, 1780-1783*. Raleigh: Edwards and Boughton, 1930.

Furneaux, Rupert. *The Pictorial History of the American Revolution as Told by Eyewitnesses and Participants*. Chicago: J. G. Ferguson, 1973.

Ganoe, William A. *The History of the United States Army*. New York: Appleton, 1924.

Garden, Alexander. *Anecdotes of the Revolutionary War in America with Sketches of Character of persons the Most Distinguished in the Southern States for Civil and Military Service*. Charleston: E. Miller, 1822.

Gelbert, Doug. *American Revolutionary War Sites, Memorials, Museums and Library Collections: A State-by-State Guidebook to Places Open to the Public*. McFarland & Co., 1998.

Gephart, Ronald M. *Revolutionary America, 1763-1789: A Bibliography*. 2 vols. Washington, DC: Library of Congress, 1984.

Gershoy, Leo. *From Depotism to Revolution, 1763-1789*. New York: Harper and Row, 1954.

Gerson, Noel B. *Light-Horse Harry*. New York: Ballantine Books, 1966.

Gibbes, R. W. *Documentary History of the American Revolution*. Columbia, SC: Banner, 1853.

Gilmore, James R. *Rear-Guard of the Revolution*. New York: Appleton, 1886.

Golway, Terry. *Washington's General:  Nathanael Geene and the Triumph of the American Revolution*. New York:  Henry Holt Company, 2005.

Goodenough, W. H., and Dalton. J. C. *The Army  Book of the British Empire*. London: 1893.

Gordon, John B. *South Carolina and the American Revolution:  A Battlefield History*. Columbia, South Carolina:  University of South Carolina Press, 2003.

Gordon, William. *The History of the Rise, Progress, and Establishment of the Independence of the United States of America*. 4 Vols. London:  Charles Dilly, 1788.

Graham, James  E. *The Life of General Daniel Morgan, of the Virginia Line of the United States, with Portions of His Correspondence Compiled from authenic Sources*. New York: Derby and Jackson, 1856.

Graham, William A. *General Joseph Graham and His Papers on North Carolina Revolutionary History*. Raleigh, NC:  Edwards and Broughton, 1904.

_____. *The Life and Character of General Nathaniel [sic] Greene.* Lincolnton, NC: The Journal Printing Company, 1901. (Address delivered in Greensboro in December 1860)

Greene, Francis Vinton. *Great Commanders, General Greene.* New York: D. Appleton and Company, 1897; reprinted by Heritage Books, Bowie, Maryland, 2002.

_____. *The Revolutionary War and the Military Policy of the United States.* New York: Charles Scribner's Son, 1911.

Greene, George Washington. *The Life of Nathanael Greene, Major-General in the Army of the Revolution.* 3 vols. New York: Hurd and Houghton, 1871.

_____. *Nathanael Greene: An Examination of Some Statements Concerning Major-General Nathanael Greene, In the Ninth Volume of Bancroft's History of the United States.* Boston: Ticknor and Fields, 1866.

Greene, Jack P., ed. *The American Revolution: Its Character and Limits.* New York: New York University Press, 1978.

_____. *The Reinterpretation of the American Revolution, 1763-1789.* New York: Harper and Row, 1968.

Greene, Jack P. and J. R. Pole, eds. *Blackwell Encyclopedia of the American Revolution.* Cambridge, MA: Blackwell, 1991.

Greene, Nathanael. *The Papers of General Nathanael Greene.* Edited by Richard K. Showman and Dennis M. Conrad. Chapel Hill: University of North Carolina Press for the Rhode Island Historical Society, 1976 to Present.

Gregg, Alexander. *History of the Old Cheraws.* Greenville, SC: Southern Historical Press, 1991.

Gregorie, Anne King. *Thomas Sumter*. Columbia, SC: R. L. Bryan Co., 1931.

Griffith, Samuel B. *The War for American Independence: From 1760 to the Surrender at Yorktown in 1781*. Garden City, NY: Doubleday, 1976.

Gwathmey, John H. *Historical Register of Virginians in the Revolution*. Baltimore: Genealogical Publishing Company1979 reprint.

Hagist, Don, N., ed. *A British Soldier's Story: Roger Lambs' Narrative of the American Revolution*. Baraboo, WI: Ballindalloch Press, 2004.

Haiman, Miecislaus. *Kosciuszko in the American Revolution*. New York: Polish Institute of Arts and Sciences in America, 1943.

Hairr, John. *Guilford Courthouse: Nathanael Greene's Victory in Defeat March 15, 1781*. Cambridge, MA: Da Capo Press, 2002.

Haller, Stephen E. *William Washington: Cavalryman of the Revolution*. Bowie, MD: Heritage Books, 2001.

Hartley, Cecil. *Heroes and Patriots of the South*; *Comprising Lives of General Francis Marion, General William Moultrie, General Andrew Pickens, and Governor John Rutledge. With Sketches of Other Distinguished Heroes and Patriots Who Served in the Revolutionary War in the Southern States*. Philadelphia: G. G. Evans, 1860.

Hatch, Charles E. Jr. *The Battle of Guilford Courthouse*. Washington, DC: National Park Service, 1971.

Hawke, David. *The Colonial Experience*. New York: Bobbs-Merrill, 1966.

Hays, Louise F. *Hero of Hornet's Nest. A Biography of Elijah Clark [sic].* New York: Stratford House, 1946.

Heitman, Francis B., ed. *Historical Register of Officers of the Continental Army During the War of the Revolution; April 1775 to December 1783.* Washington, DC: Lowdermilk, 1890.

Helsley, Alexia Jones. *South Carolinians in the War for American Independence.* Columbia: South Carolina Department of Archives and History, 2000.

Hendrick, Burton J. *The Lees of Virginia.* Boston: Little, Brown & Co., 1935.

Henry, Robert. *Narrative of the Battle of Cowan's Ford, February 1, 1871.* Greensboro: D. Schenek, 1891.

Henry, William Wirt. *Patrick Henry: Life, Correspondence, and Speeches.* 3 vols. New York: Charles Scribner's Sons, 1891.

Hibbert, Christopher. *Redcoats and Rebels: The American Revolution Through British Eyes.* New York: Avon Books, 1990.

Higginbotham, Don. *Daniel Morgan: Revolutionary Rifleman.* Chapel Hill: University of North Carolina Press, 1979.

_____. *Revolution in America: Considerations & Comparisons* Charlottesville: University of Virginia Press, 2005.

_____. *The War of American Independence: Military Attitudes, Policies, and Practices 1763-1789.* Boston: Northeastern University Press, 1983.

_____. *War and Society in Revolutionary America.* Columbia: University of South Carolina, 1988.

_____. *Atlas of the American Revolution*. New York: Rand McNally, 1974.

Higgins, W. Robert, ed. *The Revolutionary War in the South— Power, Conflict, and Leadership: Essays in Honor of John Richard Alden*. Durham, NC: Duke University Press, 1979.

Hilborn, Nat and Sam. *Battleground of Freedom: South Carolina in the Revolution*. Columbia, SC: Sandlapper, 1970.

Hill, Daniel Harvey, Jr. *Greene's Retreat*. Raleigh, NC: Capital Printing Company, 1901.

Hoffman, Paul P., ed. *The Lee Family Papers 1742-1795*. Charlottesville: University of Virginia Press, 1996.

Hoffman, Ronald and Peter J. Albert, eds. *Arms and Independence: The Military Character of the American Revolution*. Charlottesville: University of Virginia Press, 1984.

_____. et al, eds. *An Uncivil War: The Southern Back-country During the American Revolution*. Charlottesville, VA: University of Virginia Press, 1985.

Holmes, Richard. *Redcoat: The British Soldier in the Age of Horse and Musket*. New York: W. W. Norton, 2001.

Hony, Brig. Gen. P. and M. L. Weems. *The Life of Gen. Francis Marion*. Philadelphia, 1833.

Hough, Franklin B., ed. *The Siege of Savannah by the Combined American and French Forces, Under the Command of Gen. Lincoln and the Count D'Estaing, in the Autumn of 1779*. Albany, NY: J. Munsell, 1866.

_____, ed. *The Siege of Charleston by the British Fleet and Army under the Command of Admiral Arbuthnot and Sir Henry Clinton which Terminated with the Surrender of that Place on the 12th of May, 1780.* Albany, NY: J. Munsell, 1867.

Hurt, Francis Hallam. *An Intimate History of the American Revolution in Pittsylvania County, VA.* Danville,VA: Womack Press, 1976.

Huston, James A. *Logistics of Liberty: American Services of Supply in the Revolutionary War.* Cranbury, NJ: Associated University Presses, 1991.

Jameson, John F. *The American Revolution Considered as a Social Movement.* Princeton, NJ: Princeton University Press, 1926.

Johnson, Curt. *Battles of the American Revolution.* New York: Bonanza Books, 1984.

Johnson, Joseph. *Traditions and Reminiscences Chiefly of the American Revolution in the South.* Charleston: Walker & James, 1851.

Johnson, William. *Sketches of the Life and Correspondence of Nathanael Greene, Major-General of the Armies of the United States, in the War of the Revolution, Compiled Chiefly from Original Materals.* 2 vols. Charleston, SC: A. E. Miller, 1822.

Jones, Charles C. *The History of Georgia.* Boston: Houghton Mifflin, 1883.

Jones, Charles C., Jr., ed. *The Siege of Savannah, in 1779, as Described in Two Contemporary Journals of French Officers in the Fleet of Count D'Estaing.* Albany, NY: Joel Munsell, 1874.

Jones, E. Alfred and Wilbur Henry Siebert. *The Journal of Alexander Chesney: A South Carolina Loyalist in the Revolution and After*. Columbus, OH: Ohio State University, 1921.

Kajencki, Francis Casimir. *Thaddeus Kosciuszko, Military Engineer of the American Revolution*. El Paso, TX: Southwest Polonia Press, 1998.

Kapp, Friedrich. *Life of Frederich William von Steuben*. New York: Mason Brothers, 1859.

Kars, Marjoleine. *Breaking Loose Together: The Regulator Rebellion in Pre-Revolutionary North Carolina*. Chapel Hill: The University of North Carolina Press, 2002.

Katcher, Philip. *Rebels and Loyalists: The Revolutionary Soldier in Philadelphia*. Philadelphia: Atwater Kent Museum, 1976.

Kennedy, Benjamin, Ed. *Muskets, Cannon Balls and Bombs*. Savannah, GA: Beehive Press, 1973.

Ketchum, Richard M., ed. *The American Heritage Book of the Revolution*. New York: American Heritage, 1958.

_____. *Victory at Yorktown: The Campaign That Won the Revolution*. New York: Henry Holt, 2004.

Kirkland, Thomas and Robert M. Kennedy. *Historic Camden, Colonial and Revolutionary*. Columbia: The State Company, 1905.

Kirkwood, Robert. *The Journal and Order Book of Captain Robert Kirkwood*. Wilmington, DE: Historical Society of Delaware, 1910.

Lacy, Dan M. *The Meaning of the American Revolution*. New York: Oxford University Press, 1964.

Lancaster, Bruce. *From Lexington to Liberty: The Story of the American Revolution.* Garden City, NY: Doubleday, 1955.

_____. and Plumb, J. H. *The American Heritage Book of the Revolution.* New York: Dell Publishing Co, 1973.

Landers, H. L. *The Battle of Cowpens, South Carolina, August 16, 1780.* Washington, DC: United States Government Printing Office, 1929.

_____. *The Virginia Campaign and the Blockade and Siege of Yorktown, 1781.* Washington, DC: United States Government Printing Office, 1931.

Landers, Howard L. *Battle of Camden South Carolina, August 16, 1780.* Washington, DC: United States Government Printing Office, 1929.

_____. *Historical Statements Concerning Battle of Kings Mountain and Battle of Cowpens.* Washington, DC: United States Government Printing Office, 1928.

Langguth, A. J. *Patriots.* New York: Simon and Schuster, 1988.

Larrabee Harold A. *Decision at the Chesapeake.* New York: Clarkson N. Potter, 1964.

Lawrence, Alexander A. *Storm over Savannah: The Story of Count d'Estaing and the Siege of the Town in 1779.* Athens, GA: University of Georgia Press, 1951.

Leckie, Robert. *George Washington's War: The Saga of the American Revolution.* New York: Harper Collins, 1992.

Lecky, William Edward Hartpole, M. P. *The American Revolution 1763-1783: Being the Chapters and Passages Relating to America from the Author's History of England in the Eighteenth Century.* New York and London: DAppleton and Company, 1922.

Lee, Henry (Light-Horse Harry). *Memoirs of the War in the Southern Department of the United States.* Philadelphia, 1812.

_____. *The Campaign of 1781 in the Carolinas: With Remarks Historical and Critical on Johnson's Life of Greene.* Spartanburg, SC: Reprint Co., 1975.

Lefferts, Lt. Charles M. *Uniforms of the American, British, French, and German Armies in the War of the American Revolution.* New York: New York Historical Society, 1926.

Lipscomb, Terry W. *Battles, Skirmishes and Actors of the American Revolution in South Carolina.* Columbia, SC: South Carolina Department of Archives and History, 1991.

Livesey, Anthony. *Great Commanders and Their Battles.* New York: Macmillan, 1987.

Lomask, Milton. *The First American Revolution.* New York: Farrar, Straus and Giroux, 1974.

Lossing, Benson J. *The Pictorial Field-Book of the Revolution.* First Published 1851. Reprint Freeport, NY: Books for Libraries Press, 1969.

Lowell, Edward J. *The Hessians and Other German Auxiliaries of Great Britain in the Revolutionary War.* Williamstown, MA: Corner House, 1970.

Lumpkin, Henry. *From Savannah to Yorktown: The American Revolution in the South.* Columbia: University of South Carolina Press, 1981.

Mackenzie, Roderick. *Strictures on Lieut. Col. Tarleton's History.* London. 1787.

Mackesy, Piers. *The War for America, 1775-1783.* Cambridge, MA: Harvard University Press, 1964.

Maier, Pauline. *From Resistance to Revolution*. New York: Vantage, 1997.

Marshall, John. *The Life of George Washington, The Commander in Chief of the American Forces, During the War Which Established the Independence of His Country*. 5 vols. Philadelphia: C. P. Wayne, 1804 -1807.

Marshall, P. J., ed. *The Oxford History of the British Empire: The Eighteenth Century*. Oxford, England: Oxford University Press, 1998.

Marshall, Douglas W. and Howard H. Peckham. *Campaigns of the American Revolution: An Atlas of Manuscript Maps*. Ann Arbor: University of Michigan Press, 1976.

Martin, James Kirby and Mark Edward Lender. *A Respectable Army: The Military Origins of the Republic, 1763-1789*. Arlington Heights, IL: Harland Davidson, 1982.

Martin, Joseph Plumb. *Private Yankee Doodle*. Edited by George F. Scheer. Boston: Little, Brown & Co., 1962.

Matloff, Maurice, ed. *The Revolutionary War: A Concise Military History of America's War for Independence*. New York: McKay, 1980.

Mattern, David B. *Benjamin Lincoln and the American Revolution*. Columbia, SC: University of South Carolina Press, 1995.

McAllister, J. T. *Virginia Militia in the Revolutionary War*. Hot Springs, VA: McAllister, 1913.

McCall, Capt. Hugh. *The History of Georgia*. Savannah, GA: Seymour and Williams, 1811.

McCowen, George Smith, Jr. *The British Occupation of Charleston, 1780-82*. Columbia: University of South Carolina Press, 1981.

McCrady, Edward. *The History of South Carolina in the Revolution, 1775-1780*. New York: Russell and Russell, 1901.

_____. *The History of South Carolina in the Revolution, 1780-1783*. New York: Macmillan, 1902.

McCullough, David. *1776*. New York: Simon and Schuster, 2005.

McDowell, Bart. *The Revolutionary War*. National Geographic Society, 1967.

Merritt, Elizabeth, ed. *Calendar of the General Otho Williams Papers in the Maryland Historical Society*. Baltimore, MD: 1940.

Middlekauff, Robert. *The Glorious Cause: The American Revolution, 1763-1789*. New York: Oxford University Press, 1982.

Miller, John C. *Origins of The American Revolution*. Palo Alto, CA: Stanford University Press, 1943.

Miller, Nathan. *Sea of Glory: A Naval History of the American Revolution*. Annapolis, MD: Naval Institute Press, 1992.

Mitchell, Broadus. *The Road to Yorktown*. New York: McGraw-Hill, 1971.

Mitchell, Joseph B. *Decisive Battles of the American Revolution*. New York: Putnam, 1962.

_____. *Discipline and Bayonets: The Armies and Leaders in the War of the American Independence*. New York: Putnam, 1967.

Montross, Lynn. *The Story of the Continental Army, 1775-1783*. New York: Barnes and Noble, 1983.

Moore, Frank. *Songs and Ballads of the American Revolution*. New York: Appleton, 1856.

Moore, Warren. *Weapons of the American Revolution*. New York: Promontory Press, 1967.

Morgan, Edmund S. *The Birth of the Republic, 1763-89*. Chicago: University of Chicago Press, rev. ed. 1993.

_____. *The Challenge of the American Revolution*. Norton, 1976.

Morrill, Dan L. *Southern Campaigns of the American Revolution*. Baltimore, MD: The Nautical and Aviation Publishing Company of America, 1993.

Morris, Richard B. *The First Book of the American Revolution*. New York: FranklinWatts, 1956.

Morrisssey, Brandan. *Yorktown 1781: The World Turned Upside Down*. Oxford, England: Osprey Publishing, 1997 .

Moss, Bobby Gilmer. *The Patriots at the Cowpens*. Blacksburg, SC: Scotia Press, rev. ed. 1985.

Moultrie, William. *Memoirs of the American Revolution, So Far as It Related to the States of North and South Carolina and Georgia*. New York: David Longworth, 1802.

Murdoch, David H. ed. *Rebellion in America*. Santa Barbara, CA: Clio Books, 1979.

Murray, Reverend James. *An Impartial History of the War in America*. Newcastle, England: Printed for T. Robson, 1780.

Myers, Theodoras Baily, ed. *Cowpens Papers: Being Correspondence of General Morgan and Prominent Actors*. Charleston, SC: News and Courier Book Presses, 1881.

Nadelhaft, Jerome J. *The Disorders of War: The Revolution in South Carolina*. Orono: University of Maine at Orono Press, 1981.

Namier, Lewis B. *England in the Age of the American Revolution*. London: Macmillan, 1930.

Nardo, Don. *The American Revolution*. San Diego, CA: Greenhaven, 1998.

Nebenzahl, Kenneth. ed. *Atlas of the American Revolution*. Chicago: Rand McNally, 1974.

Nelson, Paul David. *General Horatio Gates: A Biography*. Baton Rouge: Louisiana State University Press, 1966.

Nelson, William H. *The American Tory*. Oxford: Clarendon Press, 1961.

Neumann, George C. *The History of Weapons of the American Revolution*. New York: Bonanza Books, 1967.

Newlin, Algie I. *The Battle of Lindley's Mill*. Burlington, NC: The Alamance Historical Association, 1975.

_____. *The Battle of New Garden*. Greensboro, NC: North Carolina Friends Historical Society, 1995.

O'Kelly, Patrick. *Nothing but Blood and Slaughter, The Revolutionary War in the Carolinas, 1780-1782*. 4 vols. Blue House Tavern Press, 2004-2005.

Oswald, Richard. *Memorandum on the Folly of Invading Virginia, the Strategic Importance of Portsmouth, and the Need for Civilian Control of the Military*. Charlottesville: University of Virginia Press for the Tracy W. McGregor Library, 1953.

Pula, James S. *Thaddeus Kosciuszko, The Purest Son of Liberty*. New York: Hippocrene Books, 1999.

Palmer, Dave Richard. *The Way of the Fox: American Strategy in the War for America, 1775-1783*. Westport, CT: Greenwood Press, 1975.

_____ and James W. Stryker. *Early American Wars and Military Institutions*. Wayne, NJ: Avery Publishing Group, 1986.

Palmer, William P., MD. *Calendar of Virginia State Papers and Other Manuscripts, 1652-1781*. Richmond, VA: R. F. Walker, Superintendent of Public Printing, 1875.

Pancake, John S. *The Destructive War: The British Campaign in the Carolinas, 1780-1782*. Tuscaloosa, AL: The University of Alabama Press, 1985.

Pearson, Michael. *The Revolutionary War*. New York: Capricorn Books, 1972.

_____. *Those Damned Rebels: The American Revolution as Seen Through British Eyes*. New York: G. P. Putnam's Sons, 1972.

Peckham, Howard H. *The War for Independence: A Military History*. Chicago: University of Chicago Press, 1958.

_____, ed. *The Toll of Independence: Engagements and Battle Casualties of the American Revolution*. Chicago: University of Chicago Press, 1974.

Peterson, Harold L. *The Book of the Continental Soldier*. Harrisburg, PA: Promontory, 1975.

Peterson, Merrill D. *Thomas Jefferson and The American Revolution*. Williamsburg, VA: Virginia Independence Bicentennial Commission, 1976.

Pickens, A. L. *Skyagunsta: The Border Wizard Owl*. Greenville, SC: Observer Printing Company, 1934.

Powell, William S. *When the Past Refused to Die: The History of Caswell County, North Carolina, 1777-1977*. Yanceyville, NC: Caswell Historical Association, 1977.

Pratt, Fletcher. *Eleven Generals: Studies in American Command*. New York: William Sloane Associates, 1949.

Purcell, L and David F. Burg, eds. *The World Almanac of the American Revolution*. New York: World Almanac, 1992.

Purvis, Thomas L. *Revolutionary America, 1763-1800*. New York: Facts on File, 1995.

Ramsay, David. *The History of South Carolina, & c*. Charleston: David Longworth, 1809.

_____. *History of the Revolution of South Carolina from a British Province to an Independent State*. 2 vols. Trenton, NJ: Isaac Collins, 1785.

_____. *History of the Revolution in South Carolina*. Newberry, SC: W. I. Duffie, 1858.

_____. *The History of the American Revolution*. Philadelphia: R. Aitken, 1789.

Randel, William Pierce. *The American Revolution: Mirror of a People*. Maplewood, NJ: Hammond, 1973.

Rankin, Hugh F. *Francis Marion: The Swamp Fox. Leaders of the American Revolution Series*. New York: Thomas Y. Crowell, 1973.

_____. *Greene and Cornwallis: The Campaign on the Carolinas*. Raleigh: NC Division of Archives and History, 1976.

_____. *North Carolina in the American Revolution*. Raleigh, NC: North Carolina Division of Archives and History, 1959.

_____. *The North Carolina Continentals*. Chapel Hill: University of North Carolina Press, 1971.

Raynor, George. *Patriots and Tories in Piedmont Carolina*. Salisbury, NC: The Salisbury Post, 1990.

Reese, George Henkle, comp. *The Cornwallis Papers: Abstracts of Americana*. Charlottesville, VA: University of Virginia Press, 1970.

Reid, Courtland T. *Guilford Courthouse*. Washington, DC: National Park Service, 1959.

Rhoads, Thomas Y. *Battle-Fields of the Revolution Comprising Descriptions of the Principal Battles, Sieges, and Other Events of the War of Independence*. Philadelphia: Bradley, 1857.

Ripley, Warren. *Battleground, South Carolina in The Revolution*. Charleston: Evening Post Publishing Co., 1983.

Risch, Erna. *Supplying Washington's Army*. Washington, DC: Center of Military History United States Army, 1981.

Ritcheson, Charles R. *British Politics and the American Revolution*. Westport, CT: Greenwood Press, 1981.

Roberts, Kenneth. *The Battle of Cowpens*. New York: Eastern Acorn Press, 1989.

_____. *The Battle of Cowpens: The Great Morale Builder*. Garden City, NJ: Doubleday, 1958.

Roberts, John M., ed. *Autobiography of A Revolutionary Soldier by James P. Collins*. North Stratford, NH: Ayer Company Publishers, Inc., 1989.

Robinson, Blackwell P. *William R. Davie*. Chapel Hill: University of North Carolina Press, 1957.

Robson, Eric. *The American Revolution in Its Political and Military Aspects, 1763-1783*. New York: W. W. Norton, 1966.

Ross, Charles, ed. *Correspondence of Charles, First Marquis Cornwallis*. London: J. Murray, 1859.

Royster, Charles. *A Revolutionary People at War: The Continental Army and American Character, 1775-1783*. Chapel Hill: University of North Carolina Press, 1979.

_____. *Light-Horse Harry Lee and the Legacy of the American Revolution*. 1994 reprint. Baton Rouge, LA: LSU Press.

Rubel, David. *America's War of Independence: 1763-1783* New York: Silver Moon Press/Agincourt Press, 1992.

Russell, David Lee. *The American Revolution in the Southern Colonies*. Jetterson, NC: McFarland & Company, 2000.

Russell, Phillips. *North Carolina in the Revolutionary War.* Charlotte, NC: Heritage Printers, Inc., 1965.

Sabine, Lorenzo. *Biographical Sketches of Loyalists in the American Revolution*. 2 vols. Port Washington, NY: Kennikat Press, 1966.

Sanchez-Saaverdra, E. M. *A Guide to Virginia Military Organizations in the American Revolution, 1779-1787*. Richmond, VA: Virginia State Library, 1978.

Sarles, Frank B., and Charles E. Shedd. *Colonials and Patriots, 1700-1783*. Washington, DC: United States Department of Interior National Park Service, 1964.

Scheer, George F. and Hugh F. Rankin. *Rebels and Redcoats: The American Revolution Through the Eyes of Those Who Fought and Lived It*. New York: DeCapo Press, 1957.

Schenck, David. *North Carolina 1780-1781 Being a History of the Invasion of the Carolinas by the British Army under Lord Cornwallis in 1780-1781*. Raleigh: Edwards & Broughton, 1889.

Schultz, Pearle H. *Generous Strangers*. New York: Vanguard, 1975.

Sellers, John R. *Manuscript Sources in the Library of Congress for Research on the American Revolution*. Washington, DC: Library of Congress, 1975.

_____. *The Virginia Continental Line*. Williamsburg, VA: The Virginia Independence Bicentennial Commission, 1978.

Selby, John E. *The Revolution in Virginia, 1775-1783*. Charlottesville: University of Virginia Press, 1988.

_____. *The Road to Yorktown*. London: Book Club Associates, 1976.

_____. *A Chronology of Virginia and War of Independence 1763-1783*. Charlottesville, VA: University Press of Virginia for the Virginia Independence Bicentennial Commission, 1973.

Seymour, William. *The Price of Folly: British Blunders in the War of American Independence*. London: Brassey's, 1995.

_____. *A Journal of the Southern Expedition*. The Historical Society of Delaware. Vol XV. Wilmington, DE: 1896.

Shaara, Jeffery. *Rise to Rebellion*. New York: Ballantine, 2002.

_____. *The Glorious Cause*. New York: Fawcett, 2003.

Sherman, William Thomas. *Calendar and Record of the Revolutionary War In the South: 1780-1781* Seattle, WA: 2003. Available free on the Internet in its entirety at http://www.americanrevolution.org/warinthesouth.html

Showman, Richard K., General Editor. *The Papers of General Nathanael Greene, Vol. VI, June-December 1780*. Chapel Hill, NC: University of North Carolina Press, 1991.

_____. *The Papers of General Nathanael Greene, Vol. VII, December 1780-March 1781.* Chapel Hill, NC: University of North Carolina Press, 1994.

_____. *The Papers of General Nathanael Greene, Vol. VIII, March -July 1781.* Chapel Hill, NC: UNC Press, 1995.

Shy, John. *A People Numerous and Armed: Reflections on the Military Struggle for American Independence.* Ann Arbor: University of Michigan Press, 1990.

Simms, William Gilmore. *The Life of Francis Marion.* New York: George F. Cooledge and Brother, 1844.

_____, ed. *The Life of Nathanael Greene.* New York: George F. Cooledge and Brother, 1849.

Smith, Page. *A New Age Now Begins: A People's History of the American Revolution.* 2 vols. New York: McGraw-Hill, 1976.

Smith, Paul H. *Loyalists and Redcoats: A Study in British Revolutionary Policy.* Chapel Hill, NC: University of North Carolina Press, 1964.

Sparks, Jared. *Correspondence of the American Revolution; Being Letters of Eminent Men to George Washington.* Boston: Little Brown and Co., 1853.

Stedman, Charles. *The History of the Origin, Progress, and Termination of the American War.* London: J. Murray, 1794; reprint, New York: Arno Press, 1969.

Stegeman, John F. and Janet A. *Caty: A Biography of Catharine Littlefield Greene.* Providence: Bicentennial Foundation, 1977; reprint Athens, GA: University of Georgia Press, 1985.

Stember, Sol. *The Bicentennial Guide to the American Revolution: The War in the South, 1780-1781*. New York: Saturday Review Press, 1974.

Stephen, Leslie and Sidney Lee, eds. *Dictionary of National Biography*. 63 vols. London: 1885-1890.

Steuart, Reiman. *A History of the Maryland Line in the Revolutionary War, 1775-1783*. Society of the Cincinnati of Maryland, 1969.

Stevens, Benjamin Franklin, ed. *The Campaign in Virginia 1781*. An exact Reprint of Six rare Pamphlets on the Clinton-Cornwallis Controversy with very numerous important Unpublished portions of the letters in their Appendixes added from the Original Manuscripts. 2 vols. London: Privately printed, 1888.

Stoesen, Alexander R. *Guilford County: A Brief History*. Raleigh: North Carolina Division of Archives and History, 1993

Stokesbury, James L. *A Short History of the American Revolution*. New York: W. Morrow, 1991.

Stone, Edwin M. *Our French Allies in the American Revolution*. Providence, RI: Providence Press, 1884.

Strieletsi, Peter. *The Outer Parallel: A Story of Nathanel Greene, Major-General in the Army of the American Revolution*. Akron, OH: Saalfield Publishing Company, 1901.

Swem, Earl G. *Maps Related to Virginia*. Richmond, VA: Virginia State Library and Archives, 1989.

Symonds, Craig L. *A Battlefield Atlas of the American Revolution*. Baltimore: Nautical & Aviation Publishing Company of America, 1986.

Tarleton, Lt. Colonel Banastre. *A History of the Campaigns of 1780 and 1781, in the Southern Provinces of North America.* London: Cadell, 1787.

Taylor, Alan. *American Colonies.* New York: Penguin, 2001.

Tebbel, John. *Turning the World Upside Down: Inside the American Revolution.* New York: Orion, 1993.

Thacher, James. *A Military Journal During the American Revolutionary War from 1775 to 1783.* Boston: Cottons & Barnard, 1827.

Thane, Elswyth. *The Fighting Quaker: Nathanael Greene.* Mattituck: Amereon House, 1972.

Thayer, Theodore. *Nathanael Greene: Strategist of the American Revolution.* New York: Twayne Publishers, 1960.

Tiffany, Osmond. *A Sketch of the Life and Services of Gen. Otho Williams.* Baltimore, MD: J. Murphy, 1851.

Tilley, John A. *The British Navy and the American Revolution.* Columbia, SC: University of South Carolina Press, 1967.

Todish, Timoth J. *America's First World War: The French and Indian War, 1754-1763.* Fleischmanns, NY: Purple Mountain Press, 2002.

Tolzmann, Don Heinrich, ed. *The Army of the American Revolution and Its Organizer: Rudolf Cronau's Biography of Baron von Steuben.* Bowie, MD: Heritage Books, 1998.

Treacy, M. F. *Prelude to Yorktown: The Southern Campaign of Nathanael Greene, 1780-1781.* Chapel Hill: University of North Carolina Press, 1963.

Trevelyan, George Otto. *The American Revolution*. New York: Longmans, Green, & Co., 1899.

_____. *George the Third and Charles Fox: The Concluding Part of the American Revolution*. New York: Longmans Green and Company, 1914.

Troiani, Don. *Soldiers in America: 1754-1865*. Mechanicsburg, PA: Stackpole Books, 1998.

Trout, W. E., III. *The Dan River Atlas. The Virginia Canals and Navigations Society and the Dan River Basin Association*, 2003.

Troxler, George. *Pyle's Massacre*. Burlington, NC: Alamance County Historical Association, 1973.

_____. *The Loyalist Experience in North Carolina*. Raleigh: North Carolina Division of Archives and History, 1976.

Turner, Joseph B., ed. *The Journal and Order Book of Captain Robert Kirkwood of the Delaware Regiment of the Continental Line*. William, DE: The Historical Society of Delaware, 1910.

Valentine, Alan. *Lord George Germain*. Oxford, England: The Clarendon Press, 1962.

Van Tyne, Claude Halstead. *The Loyalists in the American Revolution*. P. Smith, 1902; Reprint Gansevoort, NY: Corner House Historical Publications, 1999.

Uhlendorf, Bernard A., ed. *The Siege of Charleston—Diaries and Letters of Hessian Officers from the Von Jungken Papers in the William L. Clements Library*. Ann Arbor: University of Michigan Press, 1938.

Walker, Paul K. *Engineers of Independence: A Documentary History of the Army Engineers in the American Revolution, 1775-1783*. Washington, DC: United States Government Printing Office, 1981.

Wallace, David Duncan. *The History of South Carolina*. New York: The American Historical Society, 1934.

Wallace, Willard M. *Appeal to Arms: A Military History of the American Revolution*. New York: Harper, 1951.

Ward, Christopher L. *The Delaware Continentals, 1776-1783*. Wilmington, DE: The Historical Society of Delaware, 1941.
_____. *The War of the Revolution*. New York: Macmillan, 1952.

Waring, Alice Noble. *The Fighting Elder*. Columbia, SC: University of South Carolina Press, 1962.

Washington, George. *The Writings of George Washington from the Original Manuscript Sources*. Washington, DC: United States Government Printing Office, 1931-44.

Watson, Elkanah. *Men and Times of the Revolution; or, Memoirs of Elkanah Watson, Including His Journals of Travels in Europe and America from the Year 1777 to 1842*. Winslow C. Watson, ed. New York: Dana and Company, 1857.

Weigley, Russell Frank. *The Partisan War: the South Carolina Campaign of 1780-1782*. Columbia, SC: University of South Carolina Press for the South Carolina Tricentennial Commission, 1970.

_____. *History of the United States Army*. New York: Macmillan, 1967.

_____. *American Way of War: A History of the United States Military Strategy and Policy of 1780-1782*. New York: Macmillan, 1973.

Weir, Robert M. *Colonial South Carolina: A History*. Millwood, NY: KTO Press, 1983.

Weisiger, Minor T. *Using Virginia Revolutionary War Records*. Richmond: Library of Virginia, 1999.

White, Kathrine Keogh. *The King's Mountain Men, The Story of the Battle, with Sketches of the American Soldiers Who Took Part*. Dayton, VA: Joseph K. Ruebush Co., 1924.

White, Todd and Charles Lesser, eds. *Fighters for Independence: A Guide to Sources of Biographical Information on Soldiers and sailors of the American Revolution*. Chicago: University of Chicago Press, 1977.

Wickwire, Franklin and Mary Wickwire. *Cornwallis: The American Adventure*. Boston: Houghton Mifflin, 1970.

Wilcox, William B. *Portrait of a General: Sir Henry Clinton in the War of Independence*. New York: Knopf, 1962.

Wood, Gordon. *The American Revolution: A History*. New York: New American Library, 2003.

_____. *The Creation of the American Republic, 1776-1787*. Chapel Hill: University of North Carolina Press, 1969.

Wood, W. J. *Battles of the Revolutionary War, 1775-1781*. Chapel Hill, NC: Algonquin, 1990.

_____. *Leaders and Battles*. Novato, CA: Presidio Press, 1984.

Woodmason, Charles. *The Carolina Backcountry on the Eve of the Revolution & etc*. Chapel Hill: University of North Carolina Press, 1953 reprint.

Wright, Robert K., Jr. *The Continental Army*. Washington, DC: Center of Military History U. S. Army, 1983.

Wright, Stuart T. *Historical Sketch of Person County*. Danville, VA: The Womack Press, 1974.

Wrong, George M. *Washington and His Comrades in Arms: A Chronicle of the War of Independence*. New Haven, CT: Yale University Press, 1921.

## *Magazine/Journal Articles*

Aaron, Larry G. "The Race to the Dan." National Society Sons of the American Revolution. *SAR Magazine*, Fall 1995.

Anderson, Thomas. "Journal of Lt. Thomas Anderson of the Delaware Regiment." *Historical Magazine 2nd Series*.

Anonymous. "Evacuation of Charleston, S.C., 1782." *Magazine of American History* 8 (December 1882): 826-830.

Ashe, S. A. "The Battle of Shallow Ford." *Tyler's Quarterly Historical and Genealogical Magazine* 9 (July 1927): 48-51.

Ashmore, Otis, and C. H. Olmstead. "The Battles of Kettle Creek and Briar Creek." *Georgia Historical Quarterly* 10 (June 1926): 85-125.

Babits, Lawrence E. "The 'Fifth' Maryland at Guilford: An Exercise in Historical Accuracy." *Maryland Historical Magazine* 84 (1989): 371-378.

Baldwin, Samuel. "Diary of Events in Charleston, S.C., from March 20th to April 20th, 1780." *Proceedings of the New Jersey Historical Society* 2 (May 1847): 77-86.

Barnwell, Joseph W. "The Evacuation of Charleston by the British in 1782." *South Carolina Historical and Genealogical Magazine* 11 (January 1910): 1-26.

Bryant, C.B. "Notes and Queries: General J. E. B. Stuart." *Virginia Magazine of History and Biography* 12 (1905): 200-201. (Reference to Cornwallis)

Cann, Marvin L. "War in the Backcountry: The Siege of Ninety-Six, May 22-June 19, 1781." *South Carolina Historical Magazine* 72 (January 1971): 1-14.

Cashin, Edward J. "Nathanael Greene's Campaign for Georgia in 1781." *Georgia Historical Quarterly* 61 (Spring 1977): 43-58.

Clinton, Henry. "Sir Henry Clinton's *Journal of the Siege of Charleston, 1780.*" Edited by William T. Bulger, Jr. *South Carolina Historical Magazine,* 66 (July 1965): 147-174.

Clodfelter, Mark A. "Between Virtue and Necessity: Nathanael Greene and The Conduct of Civil-Military Relations in the South, 1780-1782." *Military Affairs* 52 (October 1988): 69-175.

Cole, Richard C. "The Siege of Savannah and the British Press, 1779-1780." *Georgia Historical Quarterly* 65 (Fall 1981): 189-202.

Coleman, Charles Watson, Jr., ed. "The Southern Campaign 1781 From Guilford Court House to the Siege of York, Narrated from the letters from Judge St. George Tucker to his wife." *Magazine of American History* 7 (July, September 1881): 36-46, 201-216.

Coleman, George P., Jr. "The Southern Campaign, 1781." *Magazine of American History* 7 (1881): 136-146.

Cruger, John Harris. "The Siege of Savannah 1779 As Related by Colonel John Harris Cruger." Edited by Henry C. Van Schaack. *Magazine of American History* 2 (August 1878): 489-492.

Cullen, Joseph P. "Moore's Creek Bridge." *American History Illustrated* 4 (Jan 1970): 10-19.

Davis, Robert Scott, Jr. "The Loyalist Trials at Ninety-Six in 1779." *South Carolina Historical Magazine* 80 (April 1979): 172-181.

_____. "The British Invasion of Georgia in 1778." *Atlanta Historical Journal* 24 (Winter 1980): 5-25.

_____. "Thomas Pinckney and the Last Campaign of Horatio Gates." *South Carolina Historical Magazine* 86 (April 1985): 75-99.

Dederer, John Morgan. "Making Bricks Without Straw: Nathanael Greene's Southern Campaign and Mao Tse-Tung's Mobile War." *Military Affairs* 47 (October 1983): 115-121.

De Peyster, J. Watts. "The Affair at King's Mountain 7th October 1780." *Magazine of American History* 5 (December 1880): 401-424.

Donovan, Kenneth. "John Saunders, A Loyalist Captain in South Carolina, 1780-1782." *Proceedings of the South Carolina Historical Association* (1982): 100-117.

Dunbar, Gary S. "Colonial Carolina Cowpens" in *Agricultural History*. Berkeley, California: The Agricultural History Society 35 (1961): 125-130.

Emmett, Thomas Addis. ed. "Orders Issued by Major Genl. Gates while Commanding the Southern Army, July 26th to August 31st 1780." *Magazine of American History* 5 (October 1880): 310-320.

Farley, M. Foster. "Americans Fighting Americans: Patriot vs. Loyalist at Kings Mountain, 1780." American History Illustrated 19 (1984): 30-35.

_____. "Ninety-Six in the American Revolution." *Daughters of the American Revolution Magazine* 112 (1978): 92-97.

_____. "The South Carolina Negro in the American Revolution, 1775-1783." *South Carolina Historical Magazine* 79 (1978): 75-86.

_____. "South Carolina Women in the American Revolution." *Daughters of the American Revolution Magazine* 113 (1979): 356-361.

_____. "The 'Old Wagoner' and the 'Green Dragoon.'" *History Today* 35 (1975): 190-195.

Frasché, Louis D. F. "Problems of Command: Cornwallis, Partisans and Militia, 1780." *Military Review* 57 (April 1977): 60-74.

Frink, Madge C. "A Day to Remember: October 7, 1780." *Daughters of the American Revolution Magazine* 114 (1980): 996-999.

Gaston, Joseph. "A Reminiscence of the War of the Revolution, in South Carolina." *Historical Magazine,* 3d Ser. 2 (August 1973): 90-92.

Gray, Robert. "Colonel Robert Gray's Observations on the War in the Carolinas." *South Carolina Historical and Genealogical Magazine* 11 (1910): 139-159.

Griffin, Willie Lew. "The Battle of Eutaw Springs." *South Carolina History Illustrated* 1 (1970): 24-27.

Hamilton, J. G. de Roulhac. "King's Mountain" Letters of Colonel Isaac Shelby." *Journal of Southern History* 4 (1938): 367-377.

Harden, William, ed. "Account of the Siege of Savannah, From a British Source." *Georgia Historical Society Collections* 5 (Part 1, 1901): 129-139.

Hopkins, Garland Evans. "The Life of Edward Carrington, A Brief Sketch." *Americana* 34 (1940): 458-474

Jones, George Fenwick. "The 1780 Siege of Charleston as Experienced by a Hessian Officer. Part 1." *South Carolina Historical Magazine* 88 (1987): 23-33.

_____. "The Black Hessians: Negroes Recruited by the Hessians in South Carolina and Other Colonies." *South Carolina Historical Magazine* 83 (1982): 287-302.

Kyte, George W. "The British Invasion of South Carolina in 1780." *Historian* 14 (Spring 1952): 149-172.

_____. "Victory in the South: An Appraisal of General Greene's Strategy in the Carolinas." *North Carolina Historical Review* 37 (July 1960): 321-347.

_____. "General Greene's Plans for the Capture of Charleston, 1781-1782." *South Carolina Historical Magazine* 61 (April 1960): 96-106.

_____. "Francis Marion as an Intelligence Officer." *South Carolina Historical Magazine* 77 (October 1976): 215-226.

_____. "Thaddeus Kosciuszko at the Liberation of Charleston, 1782." *South Carolina Historical Magazine* 84 (January 1983): 11-21.

Lawrence, Alexander A. "General Robert Howe and the British Capture of Savannah in 1778." *Georgia Historical Quarterly* 36 (1952): 303-327.

Lennon, Donald R. "'The Graveyard of American Commanders': The Continental Army's Southern Department, 1776-1778." *North Carolina Historical Review* 67 (April 1990): 133-158.

Massey, Gregory De Van. "The British Expedition to Wilmington, January-November 1781." *North Carolina Historical Review* 66 (October 1988): 387-411.

Mathis, Samuel. "Battle of Hobkirk's Hill." *American Historical Record* 2 (1873): 103-110.

Miller, Randall M. "A Backcountry Loyalist Plan to Retake Georgia and the Carolinas, 1778." *South Carolina Historical Magazine* 75 (1974): 207-214.

Nelson, Paul David. "Horatio Gates in the Southern Department, 1780: Serious Errors and a Costly Defeat." *North Carolina Historical Review* 50 (1973): 256-272.

Olson, Gary D. "Loyalists and the American Revolution: Thomas Brown and the South Carolina Backcountry, 1775-1776." *South Carolina Historical Magazine* 75 (1968): 44-56.

Owens, James M. "The Site of the First Eventful Failure of Lord Cornwallis." *Virginia Magazine of History and Biography* 44 (July 1936): 207-222.

Pierce, William. "Southern Campaign of General Greene 1781-2: Letters of Major William Pierce to St. George Tucker." Edited by Charles Watson Coleman, Jr. *Magazine of American History* 7 (December 1881): 431-445.

Pinckney, Thomas. "General Gates' Southern Campaign." *Historical Magazine* 10 (August 1886): 244-253.

_____. "The Revolutionary Militia in the Southern Campaign, 1780-1781." *William and Mary Quarterly*, 3d Ser. 14 (April 1957): 154-175.

Posey, John Thornton. "'The Turbulent Spirit': A Virginia Battalion in the Southern Campaign of 1782." *Virginia Cavalcade* 40 (1990): 4-13.

Rankin, Hugh F. "The Moore's Creek Bridge Campaign, 1776." *North Carolina Historical Review* 30 (January 1953): 23-60.

Robertson, Heard. "The Second British Occupation of Augusta, 1780-1781." *Georgia Historical Quarterly* 58 (Winter 1974): 442-446.

Robson, Eric. "The Expedition to the Southern Colonies, 1775-1776." *English Historical Review* 66 (1951): 535-560.

Rockwell, E. F. "The Battle of Ramsour's Mill." *Historical Magazine*, 2d Ser. 2 (July 1867): 24-27.

Rogers, George C., Jr., ed. "Letters of Charles O'Hara to the Duke of Grafton." *South Carolina Historical Magazine* 65 (July 1964).

Salley, A. S., Jr. "The Battle of Stono." *South Carolina Historical and Genealogical Magazine* 5 (April 1904): 90-94.

Shelby, Isaac. "Battle of King's Mountain October 7, 1780." Edited by J. Warren S. Dey. *Magazine of American History* 5 (November 1880): 351-369.

Skaggs, David C. "Kings Mountain and the Denouement of Southern Loyalism." *Military Review* 55 (Apr 1975): 56-60.

Smith, Derek. "Cowpens, 1781: The Defeat of 'Bloody Banny'." *Army* (Aug 1991): 40-44, 46, 48, 51-52.

Stevens, John Austin. "The Southern Campaign 1780: Gates at Camden." *Magazine of American History* 5 (1880): 241-281, 425-426.

Stoesen, Alexander R. "The British Occupation of Charleston, 1780-1782." *South Carolina Historical Magazine* 63 (April 1962): 71-82.

Tucker, St. George. "The Southern Campaign 1781 From Guilford
Court House to the Siege of York Narrated in the letters from
Judge St. George Tucker to his wife." Edited by Charles
Watson Coleman, Jr. *Magazine of American History* 7 (July,
September 1881): 36-46, 201-216.

Urwin, Gregory J. W. "Cornwallis in Virginia: A Reappraisal."
*Military Collector and Historian* 37 (Fall 1985): 111-126.

Weller, Jac. "Irregular but Effective: Partisan Weapons Tactics in
the American Revolution, Southern Theater." *Military Affairs*
21 (Fall 1957): 119-131.

_____. "Revolutionary War Artillery in the South." *Georgia
Historical* Quarterly 46 (1962): 250-273, 377-387.

_____. "The Irregular War in the South." *Military Affairs* 24 (Fall
1960): 124-136.

Wilson, John. "Lieutenant John Wilson's 'Journal of the Siege of
Charleston.'" Edited by Joseph Ioor Waring. *South Carolina
Historical Magazine* 66 (July 1965): 175-182.

### Ph.D. Dissertations

James Boone Bartholomees, Jr. "'Fight or Flee': The Combat Perfor-
mance of the North Carolina Militia in the Cowpens-Guilford
Courthouse Campaign, January to March, 1781." Ph.D.
dissertation, Duke University, 1978.

Conrad, Dennis M. "Nathanael Greene and the Southern Campaigns, 1780-1783." Ph.D. dissertation, Duke University,
1979.

Dukes, Richard Sears, Jr. "Anatomy of a Failure: British Military
Policy in the Southern Campaign of the American Revolution,
1775-1781." Ph.D. dissertation, University of South Carolina,
1993.

Grenier, John E. "The Other American Way of War: Unlimited and Irregular Warfare in the Colonial Military Tradition." Ph.D. dissertation, University of Colorado, 1999.

Ferguson, Clyde R. "General Andrew Pickens." Ph.D. dissertation, Duke University, 1960.

Konigsberg, Charles. "Edward Carrington, 1748-1810; 'Child of the Revolution'; A Study of the Public Man in Young America," Ph.D. dissertation, Princeton University, 1966.

Moss, B. G. "Role of the Scots and Scotch-Irish in the Southern Campaigns in the War of American Independence, 1780-1783." Ph.D. dissertation, University of St. Andrews, 1979.

Pugh, Robert Coplin. "The Cowpens Campaign and the American Revolution." Ph.D. dissertation, University of Illinois, 1951.

Roe, Clara Goldsmith. "Major General Nathanael Greene and the Southern Campaign of the American Revolution, 1780-83." Ph.D. dissertation, University of Michigan, 1943.

Salley, A. S., Jr. "The Georgia-Florida Campaigns in the American Revolution: 1776, 1777, and 1778." Ph.D. dissertation, Tulane University, 1979.

Scotti, Anthony John, Jr. "Brutal Virtue: The Myth and Reality of Banastre Tarleton." Ph.D. dissertation, University of South Carolina, 1995.

Searcy, Martha C. "The Georgia-Florida Campaigns in the American Revolution 1776, 1777, and 1778." Ph.D. dissertation, Tulane University, 1979.

Snapp, James Russell. "Exploitation and Control: The Southern Frontier in Anglo-American Politics in the Era of the American Revolution." Ph.D. dissertation, Harvard University, 1988.

Sull, Allan. "The Role of the Militia in the Southern States during the War for Independence, 1775-1783." Ph.D. dissertation, State University of New York at Buffalo, 1979.

Treacy, Mildred Freeman. "Nathanael Greene and the Southern Campaign: August, 1780-April 1781." Ph.D. dissertation, University of Utah, 1962.

## Master's Theses

Hoffer, Edward E. "Operational Art and Insurgency War: Nathanael Greene's Campaign in the Carolinas." Fort Leavenworth, KS: Command and General Staff College, 1988.

Jacobsen, Kristin E. "Conduct of the Partisan War in the Revolutionary War South." Fort Leavenworth, KS: United States Army Command and General Staff College, 2003.

Kennedy, Michael David. "Major General Nathanael Greene's Role in the Southern Campaign of the American Revolution, December 1780 to December 1781." Jacksonville State University, 1997.

Naisawald, Louis van Loan. "The Military Career of Robert Howe." Chapel Hill: University of North Carolina, 1948.

Smith, Michael. "Lord Charles Cornwallis: A Study in Strategic Leadership Failure." Carlisle Barracks, PA: United States Army War College, 2001.

Woodward, Joel A. "A Comparative Evaluation of British and American Strategy in the Southern campaign of 1780-1781." Fort Leavenworth, KS: United States Army Command and General Staff College, 2002.

## Books for Young People

Alderman, Clifford Lindsey. *Retreat to Victory: the Life of Nathanael Greene*. Philadelphia, PA: Chilton Books Co., 1967.

_____. *The Story of The Thirteen Colonies*. New York: Random House, 1966.

Bailey, Ralph Edgar. *Guns Over the Carolinas: the Story of Nathanael Greene*. New York: Moorow, 1967.

Bliven, Bruce. *The American Revolution*. New York: Random House, 1958.

Bobrick, Benson. *Fight for Freedom: The American Revolutionary War*. New York: Atheneum, 2004

Bodie, Idella. *The Revolutionary Swamp Fox*. Orangeburg, SC: Sandlapper, 1999.

_____. *Light-Horse Harry*. Orangeburg, SC: Sandlapper, 2004.

_____. *Heroines of the American Revolution*. Orangeburg, SC: Sandlapper 2003.

_____. *Fighting Gamecock*. Orangeburg, SC: Sandlapper, 2000.

_____. *The Wizard Owl*. Orangeburg, SC: Sandlapper, 2003.

_____. *The Old Waggoner*. Orangeburg, SC: Sandlapper, 2002.

_____. *Quaker Commander*. Orangeburg, SC: Sandlapper, 2001.

Commager, Henry Steele. *The Great Declaration: A Book for Young Americans*. Indianapolis, IN: Bobbs-Merrill, 1958.

Davis, Burke. *Heroes of the American Revolution*. New York: Random House, 1971.

Lancaster, Bruce. *The American Revolution*. Garden City, NY: Garden City Books, 1957.

Latham, Frank Brown. *The Fighting Quaker: The Southern Campaigns of General Nathanael Greene*. New York: Aladdin Books, 1953.

Lens, Sidney. *A Country Is Born: The Story of the American Revolution*. New York: Putnam, 1964.

Marshall, John. *The Life of George Washington*. Edited by Robert Faulkner and Paul Carrese. Indianapolis, IN: Liberty Fund, 2000.

Meltzer, Milton, ed. *The American Revolutionaries: A History in Their Own Words 1750-1800*. New York: Thomas Y. Crowell, 1987.

Minks, Benton and Louise Minks. *Revolutionary War*. New York: Facts on File, 2003.

Morris, Richard B. *The First Book of the American Revolution*. New York: Watts, 1956.

Orlandi, Enzo, ed. C. J. Richards, trans. *The Life and Times of George Washington*. Washington, DC: Curtis, 1967.

Peckham, Howard Henry. *Nathanael Greene, Independent Boy*. Indianapolis, IN: Bobbs and Merrill, 1956.

Schlesinger, Arthur and Meg Greene. *Nathanael Greene: Military Leader*. New York: Facts on File, 2000.

Skolnik, Richard, ed. *Our Great Heritage: The Revolutionary War Years 1763-1783*. Vol. II. New York: Consolidated Book Publishers, 1975.

## *Annotated Online References*

The following are useful websites that were operational at the time of this printing. They not only have lots of information themselves but have links to many other sites similar to the topic of discussion. Emphasis is placed on the Southern campaign.

http://www.southerncampaign.org/
> This is an online newsletter concerning all aspects of the Southern Campaign and has lots of good information and up to date articles.

http://www.cr.nps.gov/seac/
> The National Park website has a search capability, which will locate National Park sites that themselves contain valuable information about a particular battle or event. Also, the following example gives a web page with a synopsis of the Southern Campaign: http://www.cr.nps.gov/seac/socamp.htm

http://www.nps.gov/cowp/socampn.htm
> Places the Battle of Cowpens in the context of other battles in the Southern Campaign and includes helpful links, a glossary of descriptive terms, and a brief article on the Revolution as a civil war.

http://www.nps.gov/revwar/
> An excellent website emphasizing the 225th Anniversary of the American Revolution, designated *Lighting Freedom's Flame*. It includes articles on people and stories related to the war, plus a timeline offering a synopsis of major incidents. A calendar describes the Revolutionary War day by day, provides links to other Revolutionary War sites, and offers a connection to Revolutionary War Parks.

http://www.prizery.com/RacetotheDan/Exhibit.htm
> This site accesses an exhibit at The Prizery, an abandoned tobacco processing plant in South Boston, Virginia, turned Community Arts Center. The exhibit and website are working to recognize General Nathanael Greene's Crossing of the Dan

River as he retreated before Cornwallis' British army in the winter of 1781.

http://www.state.sc.us/scdah/exhibits/revolution/revsources.htm
Sources on the American Revolution from South Carolina Department of Archives and History. http://www.state.sc.us/scdah/exhibits/revolution/rvwr.pdf

http://www.pbs.org/ktca/liberty/
The Public Broadcasting System's *Liberty!* Revolutionary War documentary is featured, with outstanding graphics and articles on various aspects of the Revolution.

http://www.britishbattles.com
An interesting site which gives maps and information on battles involving British soldiers during the American Revolution and the French and Indian war.

http://www.nypl.org/
The New York Public Library, like the Library of Congress, has phenomenal resources. Even if they cannot be accessed online, the availability of resources is apparent.

www.nyhistory.org/library/resamrevgs.html
The New-York Historical Library site on American Revolution sources provides an overview of the different types of references available at similar library and university sites.

http://catalog.loc.gov/ The Library of Congress website. The following web address accesses the map site of the LOC, which has a section on Military Battles and Campaigns. http://memory.loc.gov/ammem/gmdhtml/gmdhome.html

http://www.clements.umich.edu/Webguides/Arlenes/G/GreeneN.html
Information about the collection of Nathanael Greene papers at the University of Michigan Clements Library.

http://www.army.mil/cmh-pg/books/AMH/amh-toc.htm
The Army's CMH or Center of Military History in Washington has an online version of American Military History which

covers the army's beginnings through Vietnam. The narrative covers the entire Revolutionary War and is accompanied by maps.

http://www.socialstudiesforkids.com/subjects/ushistory.htm
The site contains several pages with a narrative of the war including links to more detailed information, activities and quizzes, and a page with links to other web sites about the Revolution.

http://www.americanrevolution.com/
Lots of articles about every aspect of the Revolution accompanied by links to one another. Although the site contains little on the Southern campaign, it has an excellent and detailed timeline of the Revolutionary years as well as informative articles on topics of interest.

http://www.americanrevwar.homestead.com/files/Index2.htm
Like the previous site, this one has interesting features: quick reference articles and an index of people, places, and events important to the war.

http://www.americanrevolution.org/
Contains articles of regional interest, also on history, genealogy, and links to both British and American re-enactment groups related to the Revolution. Among the unique aspects are The Loyalists Pages, which gives that perspective on the war.

http://www.historyplace.com/unitedstates/revolution/
The years and dates of the Colonial Period through the Revolution period are indexed chronologically with a brief description of events.

http://www.sar.org/
Website for the Sons of the American Revolution, an organization of male descendants of those who served the Revolutionary cause. Descriptions of battles and stories, and a Revolutionary War calendar can be accessed.

http://ushistory.org/march/
Created and sponsored by the Independence Hall Association

in Philadelphia, site of the Independence National Historical Park.

http://www.theamericanrevolution.org/
Emphasizes important people, places, including an overview and synopsis of battles of the American Revolution.

http://www.brigade.org/
A living history organization representing British and American military groups.

http://www.libs.uga.edu/darchive/hargrett/maps/revamer.html
The University of Georgia's Hargrett Rare Book and Manuscript Library has an excellent rare map collection on the American Revolution with outstanding images.

http://jrshelby.com/sc-links/
An excellent source for all kinds of references relating to the Revolutionary War.

http://members.aol.com/JonMaltbie/NatGreene.html
A site dedicated to information about General Nathanael Greene, with a Revolutionary War chat room, and links to other sources.

http://www.banastretarleton.org
The Oatmeal for Foxhounds page provides links to other sites containing biographies, various war related documents, a "Where to Get Stuff" section, British and Loyalists perspectives plus general Revolutionary War links and a grab bag of "Just for Fun" links relating to the conflict. A great site even if you don't agree with the British view of Tarleton.

### Movies and DVDs

*1776* (Restored Director's Cut). Sony pictures, 2002.

*The American Revolution.* A & E Home Video, 2005.

*The Patriot*, starring Mel Gibson, 2000.

*The Crossing*. A & E Home Video, 2003.

*Drums Along the Mohawk* (1772) starring Claudette Colbert and Henry Fonda. 20th Century Fox, 2005.

*American Colonies/American Revolution*. Find the Fun Productions, 2005.

*Revolution* (1985) starring Al Pacino. Warner Home Video, 1999.

*Liberty—The American Revolution*. PBS, 2004.

*Founding Brothers*. A & E Home Video, 2002.

*Biography—George Washington: Founding Father*. A & E Home Video, 2004.

*The Last of the Mohicans* (1992) with Daniel Day Lewis and Madeline Stowe. 20th Century Fox, 2001.

*Rebel & Redcoats—How Britain Lost America*. PBS, 2004.

*Johnny Tremain*. Disney Studios. Originally broadcast in 1957.

Note: Older films are now on DVDs.

## *Music (CDs)*

*Colonial & Revolution Songs* by Keith and Rusty McNeil. WEM Records.

*Revolution: Songs of the Revolutionary War* by John Mock.

*Music of the American Revolution: The Birth of Liberty* by Richard Crawford. New World Records.

*The Spirit of '76 and Ruffles and Flourishes* by Frederick Fennell. Mercury.

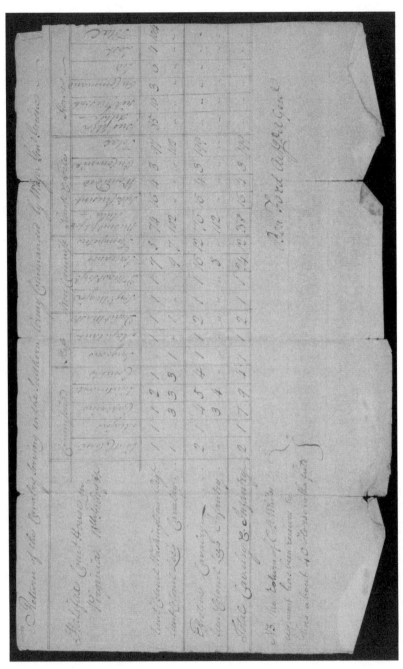

Courtesy of William L. Clements Library, University of Michigan

# Clements Library, University of Michigan

Entitled Return of the Cavalry Serving in the Southern Army commanded by Major Genl. Greene, the document on the previous page notes the location and date as "Halifax Court House February 18, 1781" and is signed by Benjamin Ford, Adjutant General. This report was prepared after General Greene's army had crossed the Dan River on February 14th and then moved his forces to Halifax County Court House.

It lists returns related to the following units: Lt. Colonel Washington's Regiment, Lt. Colonel Lee's Cavalry, plus Lt. Colonel Lee's infantry. The return gives the numbers and totals for effective cavalry and infantry for various ranks of commissioned and non-commissioned officers, staff, plus rank and file (categorized into the number present for duty, sick, and wounded). The document also lists information about the number and condition of horses.

Used by permission of the William L. Clements Library, University of Michigan.

We fight,
    get beat,
        rise and fight again.

—General Nathanael Greene

# PART IV

America must raise an empire of permanent
duration, supported upon the grand pillars of
Truth, Freedom, and Religion, encouraged
by the smiles of Justice and defended by her
own patriotic sons.

—Nathanael Greene

# Selected Dates of the American Revolution

**1754-1763**          The  French and Indian War

**1764**
April 5          The Sugar Act
Sept 1          The Currency Act

**1765**
March 22          The  Stamp Act
May 29          Patrick Henry's "If This Be Treason" speech
Oct 7-25          The Stamp Act Congress

**1766**
March 18          Repeal of Stamp Act /Declaratory Act

**1767**
June 29          Townshend Acts

**1768**          Samuel Adams' Circular Letter

**1769**
May 18          Virginia Resolutions

**1770**
March 5          The Boston Massacre

**1772**          Committees of Correspondence established
in Colonies

**1773**
Dec 16          The  Boston Tea Party

**1774**
May 20 and June 1          The Intolerable Acts
June 2          2nd Quartering Act
Sept 5-Oct 26          The First Continental Congress at Philadelphia
Minutemen organized

**1775**

| | |
|---|---|
| March 30 | New England Restraining Act |
| April 18 | Paul Revere's Ride |
| April 19 | The Battles of Lexington and Concord |
| May 10 | Fort Ticonderoga seized |
| | The Second Continental Congress in Philadelphia |
| June 15 | George Washington named Commander-in-Chief |
| June 17 | Battle of Bunker Hill |

**1776**

| | |
|---|---|
| Jan 15 | Thomas Paine publishes *Common Sense* |
| Feb 27 | Patriot victory at Moore's Creek, NC |
| March 17 | Evacuation of Boston by British |
| July 4 | Declaration of Independence |
| Aug 27-30 | British victory at the Battle of Long Island |
| Sept 15 | British occupy New York City |
| Sept 16 | British win the Battle of Harlem Heights |
| Nov 16 | British capture of Fort Washington, NY and Fort Lee, NJ |
| Dec 26 | Washington crosses the Delaware and captures Trenton |

**1777**

| | |
|---|---|
| Jan 3 | Washington's army wins the Battle of Princeton |
| Jan 6-May 28 | Washington winters in Morristown, NJ |
| Sept 11 | British victory at the Battle of Brandywine, PA |
| Sept 26 | British army under Gen. Howe occupies Philadelphia |
| Oct 4 | Battle of Germantown |
| Oct 17 | Burgoyne surrenders his British army at Saratoga, NY |

**1778**

| | |
|---|---|
| Dec 19, 1777-June 1778 | Washington's army winters at Valley Forge, PA |
| Feb 6 | France becomes ally of American Colonies |
| March 7 | General Henry Clinton becomes commander of British forces in North America |
| June 28 | Indecisive Battle at Monmouth |
| Dec 29 | British occupy Savannah, GA |

**1779**

| | |
|---|---|
| Feb 14 | Militia beat Tories at Kettle Creek, NC |
| July 15-16 | "Mad" Anthony Wayne captures Stony Point, NY |
| Aug 19 | Light-Horse Harry Lee attacks Paulus Hook, NJ |
| Sept 23 | John Paul Jones on the Bonhomme Richard captures British ship Serapis |
| Oct 9 | American attempt to recapture Savannah, GA fails |

**1780**

| | |
|---|---|
| May 12 | British capture Charleston, SC |
| May 29 | British massacre Americans at Waxhaw Creek, SC |
| July 11 | French troops arrive at Newport, RI |
| Aug 16 | British rout General Gates' Southern Army at Camden, SC |
| Sept 25 | Benedict Arnold's betrayal at West Point discovered |
| Oct 7 | Battle of King's Mountain in South Carolina |
| Oct 14 | Nathanael Greene appointed commander of the Southern Army |

**1781**

| | |
|---|---|
| Jan 1 | Unpaid Pennsylvania soldiers mutiny |
| Jan 17 | Battle of Cowpens |
| Feb 13-14 | General Greene's army Crosses the Dan River |
| March 15 | Battle of Guilford Courthouse in North Carolina |
| April 25 | Battle of Hobkirk's Hill, SC |
| June 6 | Augusta, Georgia recaptured from British |
| June 18 | Siege of Ninety-Six, SC |
| Sept 8 | Battle of Eutaw Springs, SC |
| Sept 15 | French fleet forces British naval forces from Chesapeake Bay |
| Oct 19 | Cornwallis surrenders at Yorktown, VA |

**1782**

| | |
|---|---|
| July 11 | British evacuate Savannah, GA |
| Dec 14 | British leave Charleston, SC |

**1783**

| | |
|---|---|
| Sept 3 | Treaty of Paris |
| Nov 25 | British troops leave New York |
| Dec 23 | General George Washington resigns as Commander-in-Chief |

**1787**

| | |
|---|---|
| Sept 17 | United States Constitution ratified |

Most people know of Lexington and
Bunker Hill, but very few people know that
the Revolutionary War was fought and won
in the South. The war in the South included
the bloodiest battles, the longest siege, the
worst defeat of the war, and the largest loss
of life for the French allies.

—Patrick O'Kelly, author of
*Nothing But Blood and Slaughter*

# Larry G. Aaron

The author is a native of Danville, Virginia and was graduated from George Washington High School. He received his B.S. in Biology from Virginia Tech, a B.R.E. from Midwestern Baptist College, a M.Div from Liberty Baptist Theological Seminary, and a D.Min from Luther Rice Seminary.

He has spent many years studying the Southern Campaign of the Revolutionary War, especially the Crossing of the Dan. It became a passion after he discovered that his 8th great-grandfather Abraham Aaron and his son Abraham Aaron, Jr. served in the war in the South in 1780-1781.

Aaron is founder and past president of the Dan River Chapter of the Virginia Society of the Sons of the American Revolution and past state chaplain of the Virginia Society. He is Associate Editor of *Evince*, a Dan River region arts, entertainment and lifestyle publication and has received both photography and writing awards from the Virginia Press Association.

He has been published in a variety of magazines including *Bluegrass Unlimited, Heritage Quest*, the *Magazine of History* published by the Organization of American Historians, the *SAR Magazine*, and *Blue Ridge Country*. He is also author of *Keppy's War: A Memoir of World War II* and *Barefoot Boy: An Anthology of Blue Ridge Poetry*.

Aaron is currently a teacher and chairman of the Science Department at Chatham High School in Chatham, Virginia. He resides in Danville with his wife Nancy.

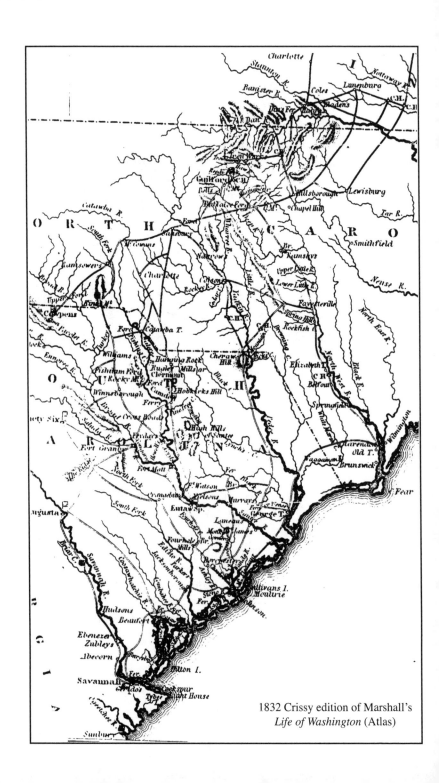

1832 Crissy edition of Marshall's *Life of Washington* (Atlas)

# INDEX

Dunmore, 43

# —Notes—